PERA PALAS

A PLAY

by

Sinan Ünel

Cover design: John Andert
www.johnandert.com
Cover photo: Pera Palas turn of the 20th century

SALT HOUSE BOOKS
info@salthousebooks.com

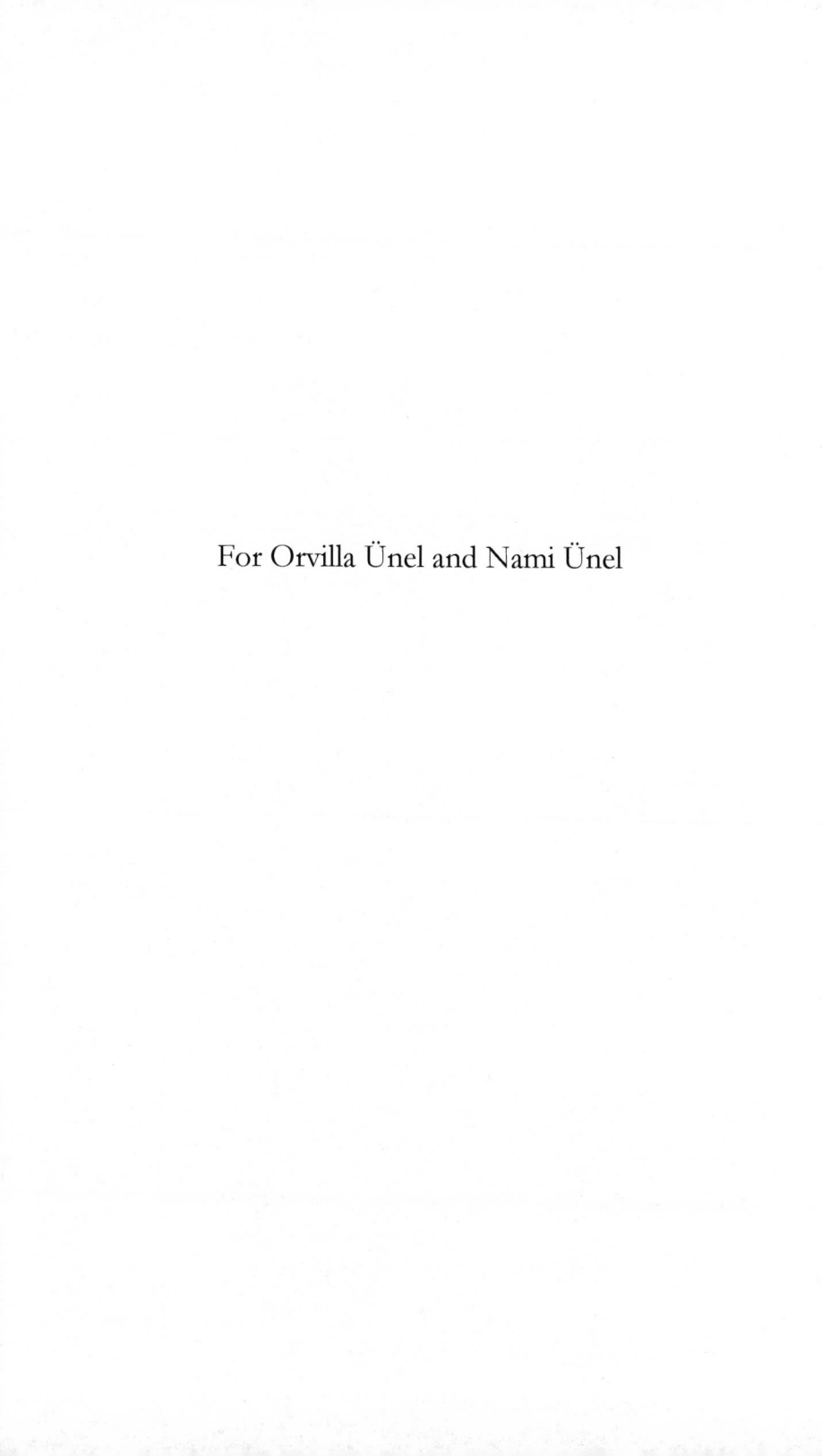

For Orvilla Ünel and Nami Ünel

ACKNOWLEDGMENTS

My deepest gratitude to The Lark Theatre and especially to my supreme collaborators John Clinton Eisner and Steven Williford for their patience, generosity and passion for the work. And John. Always John.

Pera Palas was first produced by the Lark Theatre Company at the McGinn Cazale Theater in New York City on June 11, 1998 with the following cast and creative team:

Betsy Aidem
Maggie Burke
Defne Halman
Tom Lee
Lou Liberatore
Craig Mathers
Annie Meisels
Evan Pappas
Ali Poyrazoglu
Jennifer Dorr White

Directed by Steven Williford
Set: Larry Gruber
Lighting: Howell Binkley
Costumes: by Mirena Rada
Sound: Robert Murphy
Original music: James Adler, with Scott Wilson
Production manager: Ed Teer
Production stage manager: Jennifer G. Birge
General manager: Roy Gabay
Presented by the Lark Theater Company, John Clinton Eisner,
Producing director: Lesley Malin, managing director

PERA PALAS

The play is divided into three time frames:

1918-1924

1952-1953

1994

The action develops concurrently in all three time frames.

THE SETTING

All three time frames have one common setting: a room at the Pera Palas Hotel in Istanbul. The rest of the action takes place in various settings such as the harem, the living room in 1952 or the living room in 1994. All of these settings can be suggested with a minimum amount of furniture and props.

The play is meant to flow seamlessly with instant or very short transitions between scenes. Ideally the set would allow for quick entrances and exits. The story lines should flow through each other in parallel fashion in the same space with overlapping action and dialogue.

Ten Actors are needed to play the following roles:

1918-1924:

EVELYN CRAWLEY: An English woman, about 28. A writer.

MELEK: A Turkish girl of 15.

ALI RIZA EFENDI: Melek's father. In his 60's.

JAVID: Melek's half brother, 18.

NEYME: Ali Riza Efendi's other wife, Javid's mother. In her 40's.

SIR ROBERT CAVE: An english official in his 40's.

BEDIA: A female slave, 23.

AYSHE: Ali Riza Efendi's third wife, 18.

ADALET: A guest at the harem. In her 70's.

HAREM WOMEN, SERVANTS

1952-1953:

KATHY MILLER: An American teacher, 20.

ANNE BROWN: Kathy's sister, 22.

ORHAN BAYRAKTAR: A Turkish man, 24.

JOE BROWN: Anne's husband. 25.

BEDIA OLDER: now 57

JAVID OLDER: now 52.

1994:

MURAT BAYRAKTAR: A Turkish man, 33.

BRIAN: Murat's lover, 40.

SEMA BAYRAKTAR: Murat's sister, 40.

ORHAN OLDER: Now 66.

KATHY OLDER: Now 62

KIRAZ: The maid.

THE PORTER

Five women and five men are needed to perform the following roles:

	1918-1924	1952-1953	1994
Actor 1 (f)	Evelyn		Sema
Actor 2 (f)	Melek		Kiraz
Actor 3 (f)	Neyime	Anne Osman	
Actor 4 (f)	Bedia	Kathy	
Actor 5 (f)	Ayshe	Javid Older	Kathy Older
Actor 6 (m)			Murat
Actor 7 (m)	Javid		Brian
Actor 8 (m)	Adalet	Bedia Older	Orhan Older
Actor 9 (m)	Harem woman	Orhan	Porter
Actor 10 (m)	Ali Riza Efendi Sir Robert Cave Servant	Joe Ipek	

It is important to keep in mind certain actors' doubles: The actor who plays ORHAN OLDER also plays BEDIA OLDER, his mother. The actor who plays BRIAN also plays JAVID who appears to MURAT in a dream sequence at the end of the play. Some of these are intentional, some are not, but they are significant in terms of casting, and they add an interesting angle to the script.

ACT I

In the dark we hear the ney, which is a Turkish instrument resembling the flute. On one corner of the stage, Javid Older is revealed, playing a sad tune. Evelyn appears at her desk in the hotel room, writing. It is 1918.

Evelyn: Yesterday, I arrived once again at the Queen of cities and I held my breath. As our ship anchored at the Golden Horn, I could see the seven hills, the cypress trees, and the looming minarets stretching to God like devoted believers, all bathed in those wonderful, uncertain and poetical tints which do not belong to our Western world. Nothing had changed. There was the Haghia Sophia and the majestic Süleymaniye just as I had left them. I looked upon this glorious city, my enchanting dream, with the same fascination of that school girl seven years ago.

Javid Older stops playing and leaves.

Evelyn: (cont'd) I soon discovered, however, that things had indeed changed. The war rages throughout Europe and here there is great suffering. The people are demoralized. Hunger and illness prevail and the city is overcrowded with refugees.

The door to the hotel room opens and a Porter enters with bags, followed by Murat and Brian. It is 1994. The Porter goes immediately to draw the curtains and let the sun pour in.

Brian: Man, I can't believe this place! I couldn't even grasp that lobby. All that marble and that fantastic ancient elevator!

Murat: First elevator in the city!

Brian: We're staying at a fucking palace! Would you look at this fucking room?

Evelyn: It is only here, in the district of Pera, that the ravages of war are not felt.

Murat: Built for Europeans who came on the Orient Express.

Brian: (He goes to Murat, to hug him) You didn't tell me! You bastard!

Murat: Don't touch me in front of the man.

Evelyn: For this is the district that the Europeans have adopted as their own.

Brian: Wow! The view!

Evelyn: The British, French and Italian diplomats and soldiers and their pretentious women roam about in the streets as though they are the rightful owners of this city. It is a sad, revolting sight.

Brian: I fucking feel like fucking Hercule Poirot. I'm in a fucking movie with Ava Gardner. Shit! Does he understand English?

Murat: Probably only the obscenities.

Brian: Shit. I mean oops. Sorry.

Murat: Poirot was here, of course. There's an Agatha Christie room somewhere. Some of the rooms are named after celebrities who stayed in them.

Porter: (Motioning toward the closet) Dolabiniz.

Brian: He's showing me the closet, Murat. How do you say very nice?

Murat: Çok güzel.

Brian: How do you say you're so damn cute I could die!

Murat: Çok güzel.

Brian: (Motioning quotes with his hands) Yes. "Çok güzel."

Murat: God, you're doing it again.

Brian: Sorry.

Porter: (Motioning toward the bathroom) Buyurun, banyonuzu'da göstereyim.[1]

Murat: He wants to show you the bathroom.

Brian: (To the Porter) You *are* an adorable little man.

Porter: (Bows politely) Tenk you.

Brian looks a Murat, shocked. Then he follows the porter into the bathroom.

Evelyn: As we sailed into the Bosphorus, an arrogant Englishman pointed to the two shores. See," he said, Europe and Asia, action and dreams, energy and fatalism. Liberty and bondage. I smiled as I said to myself: Poor England. The ignorance of your children is truly alarming.

Kathy enters from the bathroom in her bathrobe. 1952. She goes to the closet to pick out her outfit. Afterwards she will return to the bathroom to get dressed. Evelyn returns to her desk.

Evelyn: (cont'd) So here I am, stifled in a room of this distasteful European hotel, finding it rather impossible to write. How I hunger to enter the world of the natives and submerge myself in the luscious experience of the east.

Murat has moved to the balcony. He looks out to the city.

---

[1] Come, let me show you the bathroom

Murat: Beautiful Istanbul. Are you still mine? Will you ever be mine again?

Brian re-enters with the Porter.

Brian: Çok güzel. The bathroom is so totally "çok güzel."

Porter: (To Brian) Begendinizmi efendim?[2]

Murat: He wants to know if you like the room.

Brian: Yes, I do! I very much, very much do.

Murat reaches in his pocket to tip him.

Murat: Evet, begendik. Çok tesekkür ederiz.[3]

Brian: Tesekkür ederim.[4]

Porter: Bir sey degil, efendim.[5]

The Porter exits.

Brian: Damn! The language is such a turn-on. Tell me, tell me, tell me you gave him a fabulous tip.

Murat: I gave him an exactly adequate tip.

Brian: I hate it when you're adequate. What the hell is adequate?

Murat: Fifteen thousand.

Brian: That's... fuck you, Murat, that's fifty cents. Fifty cents!

Murat: He was pleased, I thought.

Brian: You should've given him five dollars.

---

[2] Do you like it, sir?
[3] Yes we like it. Thank you.
[4] Thank you.
[5] You're welcome sir.

Murat: That's crazy!

Brian: (He fishes for money in his wallet) For heaven's sake! The entire hotel is going to think we're Canadians.

Brian hurries out and shuts the door. Murat moves out to the balcony again, smiling. After a moment there is a frantic knock on the door. Evelyn looks up.

Evelyn: Who is it?

Melek: (Off) Êtes-vous là, Mademoiselle Crawley? [6]

Evelyn: Qui est-il s'il vous plaît? [7]

Melek: C'est Melek. Je vous en prie, ouvrez la porte, vite! [8]

Evelyn opens the door. Melek rushes inside, giggling. She is a tiny woman, covered in black and wearing a veil. Only her eyes are visible.

Melek: Oh, mon Dieu! Je suis terrifiée! [9] Quick! Shut the door before anyone sees me!

Evelyn: Are you in some trouble, Mademoiselle?

Melek: (Laughing) Not yet, thank God. But I couldn't resist, I had to do it. I was very nervous but I had to ride on that ascenseur! I have never seen such a thing! What a delightful feeling as it lifts you floor after floor after floor! My heart is racing like a horse! Feel it!

Evelyn reluctantly feels Melek's heart.

Evelyn: Forgive me for being rude, but have we met?

Melek: We met seven years ago when you were visiting with your Papa. I'm the daughter of Ali Riza Efendi. (She lifts

---

[6] Are you there, Mademoiselle Crawley?
[7] Who is it please?
[8] It's Melek. Quick, open the door, please.
[9] My God! I'm terrified.

her veil) Your friend, Melek.

Evelyn: But Melek was merely a girl. Eight years old.

Melek: But I have grown! I am fifteen and soon to be married!

Evelyn: Married?

Melek: Of course. Oh, I can't tell you how happy I am to see you. I missed you so much and I thought about you every day.

Evelyn: How did you get here, Melek?

Melek: Oh, I had to bribe Refik Aga with a song. Music is something he can never resist, the darling man. He's waiting in the carriage in the back of the hotel, nervous as a lamb at bayram. Of course I couldn't just prance right in through the front entrance.

Evelyn: Of course not.

Melek: (Giggling) You must pack your things at once! Where is your servant?

Evelyn: I'm afraid I don't have one.

Melek: But we must get you out of this dreadful place!

Evelyn: Where would I go?

Melek: To the konak, of course! You don't want to stay here all by yourself in one meager little room. There's no one to keep you company. You will stay with me at the harem!

Evelyn: At the harem? I... I don't know what to say.

Melek: Oh, please say yes! I would be so happy! We could watch the sunset every evening over the Bosphorus. And we will talk about Turkey and you will tell me all about

England and we will take walks in the garden. Please say yes!

Evelyn: (Not concealing her excitement) Yes. I would very much like that.

Melek: Wonderful! I will send a carriage first thing in the morning. But now I must leave before anyone notices me and tells Papa. I don't think I should attempt to ride the ascenseur again, don't you agree? One mustn't push one's luck.

Evelyn: Good-bye, Mademoiselle. I will see you very soon.

Melek: (Kisses her on both cheeks) I'm so glad you accepted. You'll see, we're going to be very happy together. (She puts down her veil) Like sisters.

Melek leaves the room after carefully checking the hallway. Murat goes to the phone.

Evelyn: (To the audience, very excitedly) This was beyond belief! No European that I knew had been asked to go stay in an actual harem. I was to have the opportunity to live as a real Turkish woman, to see what transpires behind those carefully guarded doors, the great mystery of the eastern world. I was so happy and terrified that I was unable to sleep that night.

Murat dials the phone, waits as it rings. Then, quickly hangs up.

Murat: Shit! Goddamnit. Shit.

In 1952, Anne opens the door and enters the room with a bag.

Anne: Kathy? Are you here?

Kathy: (From the bathroom. Lightheartedly) Hi. You're late. I was about to get worried.

Anne: The train was late. The Turks are definitely not familiar with the notion of punctuality. The man who sat next to me kept saying, "why are you in such a hurry? Your destination won't walk away."

Exhausted, she throws down her bag and falls in the chair.

Anne: Imagine if all Americans felt that way. Chaos!

Kathy: (Enters, laughing, combing her hair) You don't sound like you had such a great trip.

Anne: (Takes off her shoes) It was fine. Of course Joe's miserable.

Kathy: How come?

Anne: He's just homesick, that's all. Baseball, hot-dogs, the usual. Can I take a quick shower before dinner?

Kathy: (Going back to the bathroom) Sure. I'll be finished in the bathroom in a minute.

Anne begins to undress. Brian re-enters.

Brian: Greta Garbo in 503, Mata Hari in 504. Fucking Mata Hari, right down the hall. And I always thought she was fictional.

Kathy: (From the bathroom) I'm not having dinner at the hotel tonight.

Anne: Oh, really? How come.

Kathy: I have a date.

Anne: What?

Kathy: I said, I have a date.

Brian: Our room is called the Evelyn Crawley. Who I have no idea who that is.

Murat: Sounds English. Probably some obscure writer or diplomat's wife.

Brian comes out to the balcony.

Brian: Don't you want your camera?

Murat: I'm not ready.

Brian: Even the smog has a certain exotic charm. What color is that exactly? (Quoting with his fingers) "Chartreuse?"

Murat: Do you have any idea how annoying that is?

Brian: Sorry. Here break my fingers, all of them. (He holds out his fingers. Murat kisses them) What's that amazing dome?

Murat: The great Suleymaniye mosque.

Brian: And that one over there?

Murat: The Haghia Sophia. And curving through is the Golden Horn. Because everything that glitters in Turkey is golden.

Brian: It's like nothing's changed in centuries.

Murat: Yeah, except another bridge over the Bosphorus and McDonalds every few blocks.

Brian: Oh, I know. I hate that.

Murat: That's not true. You love McDonalds.

Brian: But not here! Here I want to be in a dream. Where time stands still.

Murat: It's alright. The essence is the same.

Kathy enters. She picks up a letter and hands it to Anne.

Kathy: Oh. I almost forgot. We got this today.

Anne takes the letter, looks at her. Kathy returns to the bathroom. Anne reads.

Murat: Come on, let's go get something to eat.

Brian: But you haven't called your parents yet.

Murat: Later.

Brian: What do you mean? Aren't they waiting by the phone or something?

Murat: Not really. Come on. I'm starving.

Brian: Wait. They know we're coming today, right?

Murat: No.

Brian: You didn't tell them?

Murat: No.

Brian: Why not?

Murat: I just didn't.

Murat goes to the bathroom as Kathy reenters.

Anne: Poor Mom. She's worried about us.

Kathy: She's worried about everything. I wouldn't have been able to step outside the state if it weren't for you and Joe.

Anne: You should write to her this time. I've written to her every week.

Kathy: Please, Anne. Writing letters gives me a nettle rash.

Kathy sits at the vanity to apply make-up. Anne continues to read. Murat enters.

Brian: Okay, what's this all about? Do they know we're

coming at all? When are you gonna call them?

Murat: I haven't decided.

Brian: What's that supposed to mean?

Murat: Sorry, let me rephrase that: I haven't decided.

Brian: Not even your sister?

Murat: If I told her my parents would know too, now, wouldn't they? Come on, I'll buy you the best lunch of your life.

Brian: Murat...

Murat: (Grabs Brian by the waist) Authentic Turkish street food. You'll love it.

Brian: I don't think so.

Murat: Come on. Be a little adventurous. Let's have some fun.

Brian: Right in the city where you lost your authentic Turkish chastity. Probaby a hundred times.

They exit.

Anne: (Folding the letter) Who do you have a date with, Kathy?

Kathy: (Lightheartedly) A young man I met.

Anne: Met where?

Kathy: At the school, of course. Where else do I go? He made an appointment to talk about his sister. I thought that was very responsible of him. Mother would like that. When you write to her about it, that is.

Anne: Do you want me to write to her about it?

Kathy: (Kidding her) Come on, Anne. Don't act like such a big sister.

Anne: What's his name?

Kathy: Orhan.

Anne: A Turkish man?

Kathy: (Putting on lipstick) Yep.

Anne: (Pause) Are you sure this is a good idea?

Kathy: Listen to you. You're talking just like Mother.

Anne: We've only been here a couple of months. You know hardly anything about these people.

Kathy: (Checking herself in the mirror) These people?

Anne: The Turks! Don't you think you should *know* more about these people's culture before you go out on a date with one of them?

Kathy: Joe's the one who's making you think that way. The man nearly soiled his pants when he was told he'd been given a foreign assignment. And it wasn't England and not even France!

Anne: Don't talk about him like that....

Kathy: (Quickly) I'm sorry, I didn't mean...

Anne: He's been nothing but kind to you. He treats you like his own sister.

Kathy: What do you expect, Anne? Should I not talk to anyone? You and Joe have each other and I don't have any friends of my own. So far the only places I've been are the school and the grocery store on the corner. I want to see the city, I want to meet some new people. Aren't you a bit curious?

Anne: Not really. I'm cautious, that's all. You just fling yourself into situations without even thinking.

Kathy: Look. It's just an innocent meeting. He said he would show me the city. Will you please not worry about me?

Anne: Don't be late.

Kathy: (Kisses her) I won't.

Kathy leaves as Evelyn appears, dressed in street clothes and a hat.

Evelyn: Early the next morning, Refik Aga, who could not look at my face for fear of seeing a strand of my hair, took me in his carriage to the konak. I recognized it as the house I had been to when I was with my father. The large dwelling is divided into two sections. This I knew and expected, of course. The harem for the women and the selâmlik for the men. A man, unless he is a husband or small boy, is forbidden to enter the harem at all times. And the women have access to the selâmlik only through the unfortunate invention called the lattice, more commonly referred to as the cage. In other words, they are allowed to look, but not be seen or heard.

She is greeted by Melek who shrieks with delight and kisses her on both cheeks.

Melek: I'm so happy you're here. I will take you to your room right away so you can settle and change.

They enter Evelyn's room where they are met by Bedia, an odelisque. Bedia is shy and looks only at the floor.

Melek: (cont'd) This is Bedia. She is to assist you. She will bring you to the salon when you're ready. Don't be long, my darling, we're all waiting anxiously.

Melek leaves. Evelyn looks out the window. Bedia immediately starts to undress her.

Evelyn: My room is large and manifests a breath-taking view of the Bosphorus. The odelisque assigned to me speaks no English or French but is very eager to please. Melek has told me that each year Bedia is asked whether she would like to marry and leave this house but so far she has refused. I understand immediately that her utmost duty is to never, under any circumstances, allow me to do anything without her assistance. (To Bedia) Teşekkür ederim, Bedia. (Bedia helps her slip into harem clothes) She bathes me, dresses me, brings me tea and sherbet. And if there is nothing urgent left to do, there is always the endless brushing of my hair. I do wish she would give me my privacy if only for a few minutes but to no avail. She is a charming girl and she and I seem quite stuck together. (Again, to Bedia) Teşekkür ederim.

Bedia quickly goes to the vanity and takes a box and opens it to show its contents.

Evelyn: (cont'd) My goodness! I have never seen such beautiful stones! (Bedia tries to put a bracelet on Evelyn) But I couldn't. (Bedia looks at her, puzzled) They're not mine.

Bedia: (She manages to attach the bracelet) Çok güzel, çok güzel.

Evelyn: Yes, they are beautiful, but I can hardly believe they were left for me to... (To the audience, as Bedia also puts a necklace on her) ...they were left for me to wear, all these diamonds and rubies. Even my brush and comb were gilded with gold. I have never witnessed such dazzling opulence. And I am amazed at the degree of trust invested in the servants of this house who appear not to even dream of stealing anything.

Bedia admires her for a moment.

Evelyn: (cont'd) Alright, we can go.

They enter the salon, or the living area of the harem. The room is lined on the sides with bench-like couches covered with expensive material and pillows, for the women to recline upon. In the middle of the room there is a mangal, which is an ornate round coal stove made of brass. There are several women, most of them guests, and several concubines. The women are dressed in Turkish clothes of the period and wear expensive jewels. Aside from gossip and usual affection among the women, the main occupations of the harem are smoking, eating, drinking and embroidering, all done in great luxury and comfort. Coffee and sherbet are served every few minutes.

Ayshe: Adalet Teyze, did you see the woman? My God. She's taller than a pine tree.

Melek: But her clothes are so beautiful.

Ayshe: She prances around with that shapka like a tea tray on her head.

The women laugh as Ayshe does a comic imitation of Evelyn. Evelyn enters with Bedia.

Melek: Welcome, my darling! Come, make yourself at home.

Melek leads Evelyn to meet some of the women.

Melek: This is Neyime. She's my father's first wife.

Neyime: Trés heureuse, Mademoiselle, a faire votre connaissance.[10]

---

[10] Very nice to meet you, Mademoiselle

Evelyn: Bonjour, Madame.

Melek: Neyime has been like a mother to me since my own mother's death.

Neyime: You flatter me, my dear. No one can take the place of one's own mother.

Melek: And this is Ayshe, my father's third wife.

Ayshe is young, shy and giggly.

Evelyn: Bonjour, Madame.

Ayshe: (Giggling awkwardly) Bonjour.

Melek: I'm afraid her french is dreadful. She was an odelisque at the Sultan's palace before my father married her and she's an excellent musician.

An older woman, Adalet, speaks from a corner where she is reclining and smoking.

Adalet: Sor bakalım Melek, neden evli değilmiş?[11]

Melek: That's Adalet hanım. She came for lunch ten years ago and hasn't left since!

Evelyn: What is she saying?

Melek: She wants to know why you haven't married.

Evelyn: Tell her it's because I value my independence.

Melek: (To Adalet) Istiklâlimi tercih ederim diyor, Adalet teyze.[12]

Adalet: Istiklâlmi? Salak gâvura bak.[13] (Laughs. To the other

---

[11] Ask her, Melek. Why isn't she married?
[12] She says she values her independence, aunt Adalet.
[13] Independence? What a silly infidel.

women) She says she likes her independence. It's because their men are no good in the bedroom. Why else would a pretty thing like that still be a virgin at her age?

Neyime: Europeans are so strange.

The other women react and talk in Turkish.

Evelyn: What are they saying?

Melek: You mustn't mind them. They will always find something to talk about.

Melek spots Javid sneaking into the harem.

Melek: (cont'd) Oh, and this... (to Javid, calling him in) Gel, gel, utanma.[14] (to Evelyn)...this is my half brother Javid. Neyime's son. He's not allowed in the harem anymore but Neyime lets him visit from time to time.

Evelyn: Bonjour, Javid.

Javid: Bonjour, Mademoiselle.

Adalet: Sor balakım Melek. Shapkayı sor.[15]

Melek: (She laughs with the other women) She wants to know if she goes to England, will they make her wear a hat too?

Lots of giggling.

Evelyn: I suppose they would, wouldn't they.

The women laugh, although they don't understand her.

Melek: (To Adalet) Evet, giydirirler diyor.[16] (To Evelyn) Adalet Teyze will never go. She's terrified of hats. She

---

[14] Come, come. Don't be shy.
[15] Ask her about the hat, Melek.
[16] Yes, she says they will.

thinks they are hideous.

Evelyn: (To Adalet) They really are, aren't they? I'm terrified of them too.

The women all laugh.

Melek: Come, I want to show you the garden.

Evelyn and Melek exit.

Ayshe: I pity European women. Who would want independence when one can have a husband and her own children.

Javid: I like her. I think she's right to want her freedom.

Adalet: Be quiet, Javid. Can't you see we're pretending you're not here? A grown son in a harem, Neyime. Who's ever heard of such a thing?

Neyime: She's right, Javid. You should leave now.

Adalet: Let him stay, for the love of Allah. He's harmless and he misses his mother. Don't just sit there, boy, play something.

Javid plays the ud. Lights dim over the harem. Kathy and Orhan are on the deck of a boat on the Bosphorus. Sounds of horns and seagulls. It is a moonlit night. They find a bench to sit, looking out to the European shore. They have small glasses and a flask of raki, a very strong alcoholic drink.

Orhan: This is a good spot. Away from the wind. Are you comfortable?

Kathy: Yes. It's so beautiful.

Orhan: There is nothing like being on the Bosphorus on a boat on a moonlit night. Look. That's the palace built by the last Sultan. Atatürk died there...Cigarette?

Kathy: Why not?

Orhan: (Looking out to the shore)No one, in all of history, has ever achieved the reforms made by Atatürk. Like a magician, he took a dying, medieval country and transformed it into what Turkey is today.

Kathy: It's fantastic.

Orhan: Yes. A miracle. He abolished polygamy. He created a secular constitution and gave women their freedom. Today we have women judges and doctors and... you're not drinking. Is there something wrong with your drink?

Kathy: (Laughs) No. I just think I'm getting a little drunk. And this cigarette is making me dizzy.

Orhan: Would you like me to take you back to the hotel?

Kathy: (Slightly dazed) No! No, I'm fine, really.

Orhan: Look, the seagulls are flying low. It means there is going to be a storm.

Suddenly he leaps onto the railing, hanging off a pole, laughing. Kathy screams.

Orhan: (cont'd) Did you know that we had our first beauty contest only this past summer?

Kathy: Oh, God! What are you doing? Come down!

Orhan: Twenty-five years ago women weren't allowed to expose their hair or the skin on their arms.

Kathy: (over) Orhan! Come down, you're scaring me! Come down!

Orhan: Now we see pictures of them in bathing suits on the front pages of newspapers. Posing!

Poses ridiculously, hanging over the water. Kathy screams.

Then, calmly, and suddenly seriously, he comes off the pole, sits next to her. She breathes, still in shock.

Orhan: (cont'd) I know it's silly but it brings tears to my eyes. Everything you see in Turkey today is one great man's accomplishment of an impossible dream. We're very proud of that.

He looks out to the water, inhales, filling his lungs with salty air. Then turns to her. She's staring.

Orhan: (cont'd) Why are you looking at me that way?

Kathy: I don't know. I didn't realize I was looking.

Orhan: (Laughs) You are a little drunk, eh?

She looks down, embarrassed. He lifts her chin with his finger and looks into her eyes.

Orhan: (cont'd) You have pretty eyes. I like it when you look at me.

Kathy: You're pretty neat yourself.

She laughs at her own drunken Americanism.

Orhan: And it's lovely when you laugh.

He takes her hand and kisses it, holds it against his face. She is mesmerized.

Orhan: (cont'd) Come on. Let me take you to the other end of the boat. I'll show you the Asian side. Perhaps it will strike you as humorous as the European side.

Kathy: It's getting kind of chilly, isn't it?

Orhan: Here, I'll give you my coat.

Kathy: (As he drapes his coat on her shoulders) But then you will be cold.

Orhan: Oh, no. Your presence will keep me warm.

He puts his arm around her and they walk off. A the harem, Javid plays the ud. Melek is teaching Evelyn embroidery. Neyime looks out the window longingly, listening to the melancholy tune, watching the boats sail by on the Bosphorus.

Evelyn: I give up, Melek. I have no talent for this sort of thing.

Melek: You are so impatient with yourself! Do you think I learned embroidery in one day?

Evelyn: He plays so beautifully, that Javid.

Melek: Yes. Loves the music of Europe as well. His greatest dream is to hear Wagner performed by a full orchestra.

Evelyn: And what is your dream, Melek?

Melek: Of course to be married and have beautiful children. And I would like to have dinner in a restaurant some day.

Evelyn: But I can take you to a restaurant here in Constantinople.

Melek: Goodness! We could never do that, two women walk into a restaurant. We would be asked to leave and if Papa heard about it, he would kill me!

Bedia: (Enters, rushing) Beyefendi geliyor, Melek sultan.[17]

Melek: There's Papa coming now.

All the women, except Melek and Neyime pull down their veils.

Bedia: (Going to Evelyn to cover her face) Javid, you must leave!

Melek: Don't say a word like that in front of him.

---

[17] The master is coming, Sultan Melek.

Evelyn: (Removing the veil) Thank you, I don't need that, Bedia. Ali Riza Efendi has seen my face many times.

Javid tries to leave quickly but Ali Riza Efendi has entered the room. Melek rushes to him quickly.

Melek: Hello, Papa!

Ali Riza Efendi: How is my little robin today? I haven't heard your beautiful voice in so long.

Melek: I will sing for you anytime, Papa, you know that.

Javid is sneaking out. Ali Riza sees him.

Ali Riza Efendi: Javid! Stop!

Melek: He was just leaving, Papa. Don't be angry at him.

Ali Riza Efendi: What are you doing here? How do you explain yourself?

Neyime: It's my fault, Ali Riza. I allowed him to come.

Ali Riza Efendi: Get out at once!

Javid runs out. To Neyime.

Ali Riza Efendi: How many times have I told you. You're spoiling the boy! (He sees Evelyn) Ah, Mademoiselle Crawley. How nice to see you again. Are you enjoying your stay?

Evelyn: Yes, very much, thank you. Melek and I spend a great deal of time talking.

Ali Riza Efendi: How very nice. However, you must want to see some of your countrymen on occasion, am I right?

Evelyn: Not very much, thank you.

Ali Riza Efendi: There is a gathering at the Italian consulate

Tuesday evening. I would so much appreciate it if you would accompany me.

Evelyn: I'm grateful for the invitation, Ali Riza Efendi, but wouldn't you like to take...er, one of your wives?

Ali Riza Efendi: Oh, no. They do not enjoy the company of men, especially not diplomats. You, on the other hand, have an interest in politics.

Melek: Do go, Evelyn. You would enjoy it and afterwards you could tell me all about it.

Ali Riza Efendi: I hope you won't think me rude for insisting, Mademoiselle. As a member of the ruling family, it would make a nice impression if I were accompanying an English woman of your distinction.

Melek: Go, Evelyn, go!

Evelyn: If it would be of any help, Monsieur, I would be happy to come.

The hotel room. Late night. Murat and Brian enter.

Brian: I'm sorry, those waiters wanted me. They all wanted me *so* bad.

Murat: You're so dreaming that it's pathetic.

Brian: Man. I haven't had this much fun since I've been sober.

Murat: I still don't believe you forced the entire staff of them to dance with you. Suddenly there it was in front of my very eyes, the thing I've feared the most: my boyfriend as Snow White and the seven dwarfs. Humiliating.

Brian: You have no clue. Turkish men are thoroughly

evolved about homosexuality.

Murat: Of course they are! You kept tipping them obscene amounts of money.

Brian: They're hugging and kissing, always holding hands on the street, it's amazing.

Murat: You've got to travel more.

Brian: Come here.

Murat: Not right now.

Brian: You're so uptight.

Murat: I worry about you. Just tell me. Are you okay?

Brian: What was that stuff you made me eat? Kokoreç.

Murat: I told you seven million times: it wasn't liver.

Brian: Why won't tell me what it was?

Murat: Because I can't feed you exotic and delicious things if you won't eat anything exotic and delicious. You wouldn't even eat your fish and we eat fish all the time in America.

Brian: Fish in America don't glare!

Murat: I just asked you a question. Why won't you answer me.

Brian: It's been two years, Murat, I think I can handle it by now.

Murat goes to the balcony.

Brian: (Following him) What's the matter, my sullen sheikh? Did I embarrass you?

Murat doesn't answer.

Brian: I can learn to be Turkish, you know. We could live here, don't you think? You could take all your gorgeous pictures and make your book and I'd be in tile heaven.

Murat: I'm not making a book.

Brian: Come on, Murat. You have to talk to me.

Murat: I'm fine.

Brian: You haven't let me touch you in three days. You mope in the streets like you lost something, your camera dangling from your neck, not taking a single photograph.

Murat: I keep asking myself, why did I come? I thought I'd find some relief.

Brian: You have to call them.

Murat: I know that. Don't you think I know that?

Brian: Do it now.

Murat: It's late. In the morning.

Brian: You're lying.

Murat: I can't do it!

Brian: Three more days, Murat. Three. Family's all we've got.

Murat: This is a mistake. I can't believe I'm making the same stupid assumptions.

Brian: You're a thickheaded, proud prick, you know that? You won't pick up that phone because of God knows what happened nine years ago. I swear breeders should not be allowed to raise their own kids. They just fuck everything up.

Murat: Okay, okay...

Brian: And furthermore, on an infinitely more selfish note, I'm not at all thrilled about not getting any. I'm going to bed.

Murat: Brian, please...

Brian: Hey! Don't come near me now cookie. I'm no longer in the mood.

Suddenly Brian keels over in pain

Brian: (cont'd) Ow! Ow! My God!

Murat: (Running to him)What's the matter? What's wrong?

Brian: Get me to the bathroom. Quick, get me to the bathroom!

Murat rushes him to the bathroom. At the harem, Evelyn enters her room. It is dark. Bedia is asleep. Evelyn tries not to wake her. Melek appears at the door.

Melek: Evelyn.

Evelyn: Oh! You startled me, Melek.

Bedia wakes.

Evelyn: (cont'd) I'm sorry, Bedia. Go back to sleep.

Melek: It's alright. She can sleep elsewhere. (To Bedia) Git Bedia, başka yerde uyu.[18]

Bedia scurries off.

Evelyn: What are you doing up so late?

Melek: I waited for you. I wanted to hear all about the ball.

Evelyn: Oh, it was miserable. The people were more pretentious than I even remembered them. I'm afraid I'm

---

[18] Go Bedia, sleep somewhere else.

becoming a Turkish woman, Melek. I see no pleasure in dancing with strangers at a ball.

Melek: Was Ali Shevket Efendi there?

Evelyn: I don't think so. Who is he?

Melek: He's the man I am to marry. Was there a great deal of dancing?

Evelyn: Oh, yes.

Melek: Papa loves to dance. Did you dance with him?

Evelyn: I'm afraid I'm not as good a dancer as he, but yes, to his chagrin, I did.

Melek: (Jumps on the bed) Tell me, tell me all about it. What were the women wearing?

Evelyn: No. Now it is my turn to ask some questions, Melek.

Melek: Questions about what? What answers could I possibly have for you?

Evelyn: How could you marry a man you have never met?

Melek: But that's the way we do things here. It's our custom.

Evelyn: When I look at Neyime, I see how sad she always is. It must be terrible to have to share your husband with another woman.

Melek: Neyime's given my Papa a beautiful son. That's all that matters to her. She and Ayshe are like sisters. Besides, that's not done anymore. Things are changing.

Evelyn: What if he's not a good man. What if you don't like him.

Melek: Papa would never make me marry a bad man or a

man who is ugly or old. I trust Papa. You should talk to Javid. He goes to those meetings where they discuss the issues of women in Turkey and how things should change and that sort of thing.

Evelyn: Wouldn't you like to go?

Melek: Goodness, no. I have no interest. Javid says all the women sit in their veils while the men stand up and make speeches. I would hardly call that a women's meeting. I'm much happier staying at home and embroidering. Javid told me Halide Hanim is always there but I don't like her. Papa says she's a progressive. (Reclining on the bed) Now tell me all about England that I always dream about and that I will never see.

The hotel room is dark. Kathy enters quietly. She's been drinking. Anne is waiting for her, sitting in the dark.

Anne: Hello.

Kathy: (Trying not to show her drunkenness) What are you doing up?

Anne: I woke up and you still weren't here. It's almost morning.

Kathy: I'm sorry. Were you worried?

Anne: You've been very busy lately, Kathy. I've hardly seen you in the last few days.

Kathy: (Meekly) I know. I'm sorry.

Anne: I know about this fellow Orhan. I talked to the headmistress today. Many people know him.

Kathy: Why on earth did you talk to her?

Anne: Apparently he's been involved with many girls, your young man. I should say women, young ones and old ones and...

Kathy: (Over) Oh, come on, Anne...

Anne: (Over) ...even married women. Did you know that?

Kathy: No. But I'm grateful that you have found it out for me.

Anne: You're out of your mind to get involved with such a creep.

Kathy: (Angrily) He's not a creep! Of course he's dated a lot of girls, he's very handsome, why not? But this is different. He feels differently about me.

Anne: (A light chuckle) Do you believe him when he tells you that?

Kathy: Shut up, Anne. You haven't even met him...

Anne: Don't talk to me like that! You're drunk!

Kathy: He comes from one of the most reputable families in Istanbul. He has a promising career. He has ideals, he has purpose, he wants to do something with his life.

Anne: You've been out with him every night this week. You don't get home until the early morning and when you do you smell of alcohol and cigarettes.

Kathy: I'm in love with him!

Anne: (Pause) Well. That was fast.

Kathy: I can't help it.

Anne: Fine. That does it.

Kathy: What?

Anne: I'm going to tell Miss Hattersley that you won't be renewing your contract for next semester.

Kathy: What?

Anne: You'll be back home in time for Christmas.

Kathy: You can't do that!

Anne: You had this in mind all along, didn't you? Some Arabian Nights fantasy, being swept off your feet by a handsome, no-good foreigner. I should never have brought you. I thought you had more sense than this.

Kathy: You will not send me back. I will not go back to that house and live with that stubborn, old, unhappy woman!

Kathy goes to the bathroom, slams the door. Brian comes out of the bathroom. Murat is sitting on the balcony.

Brian: Man, I've never had such diarrhea. I think I drowned the fucking bathroom.

Murat: I'm sorry.

Brian: You're sorry? I hope *you'll* never know the meaning of utter intestinal collapse in a building with precarious plumbing. You're not gonna to cure me by staying up all night, you know. Get some sleep.

Murat: I'm not sleepy.

Brian: I shudder at the thought but I suppose I should know.

Murat: No, you shouldn't.

Brian: Come on, come on, you can tell me. I won't to be mad.

Murat: No, I can't, and oh, yes, you will.

Brian: Murat. You don't have the strength of character to face what I'm capable of producing right now, right here, on this bed. Nor do you have the fortitude to clean it up. Now what did you feed me?

Murat: They were...

Brian: What? They were what? Will you tell me before I'm dead?

Murat: Intestines.

Brian: Come again?

Murat: Lamb intestines. I'm sorry. I didn't think they'd make you sick.

Brian: Oh, my God. What's wrong with you? I should've listened to my mother. Men are snakes!

Murat: Brian, Brian, please...

Brian: He's trying to poison me, Ma! Intestines! For heaven's sake, what kind of people eat intestines?

He returns to the bathroom, slams the door.

Murat: I'm sorry. I didn't know. I'm so sorry, Brian. Forgive me, please.

Melek: Papa has great reverence for everything British. He thinks the British are wise and they see very far. They are just and understand the idea of liberty.

Murat moves to the bathroom door, leans against it.

Murat: Brian?

Melek: We have implicit confidence in what they do.

Murat: Brian?

Brian: What could you possibly want right now?

Murat: Can I come in?

Brian: Yeah, sure! Clearly this entire trip is about humiliating Brian.

Murat: I did it because... because you've been so cautious lately. You won't take any risks, you won't do anything out of the ordinary...

Brian: I used to when I was a drunk, you asshole! Is that what you want me to be again?

Murat moves away from the bathroom door. We hear the call to prayer. Kathy comes out of the bathroom.

Melek: It's dawn. Time passes so fast when I talk to you.

Anne: The sun is up. You didn't get any sleep.

Kathy: I will. I don't have class until the afternoon.

Melek: However, I don't think I would like to be an English woman. English women work and I don't know how to work.

Anne: Fine. I'm going downstairs for breakfast. I'll see you at the school.

Evelyn: In many ways it is much more difficult to live the English woman's life.

Kathy: He loves me, Anne. Why can't you be happy for me for once?

Anne exits room. Brian enters.

Brian: I can't sit in there listening to this. It's so fucking ominous.

Murat: I'll go get you some breakfast.

Brian: Ha, ha. That's very funny Murat. I didn't know you had a sense of humor all of a sudden.

Murat: Sorry.

Brian: I just want to get some sleep. You go. Go, go, go!

Murat: (Starts to leave, then stops) Brian...

Brian: What?

Murat: I've been thinking about it all night.... I'm not going to call them. It's not worth it. I just want to be with you. I don't want anything to fuck that up.

Brian: And what if I called them?

Murat: What?

Brian: You're a coward, Murat.

Murat: You wouldn't do that.

Brian: Are you taking your camera? Take your camera.

Murat takes the camera.

Btian: (cont'd) And be careful out there.

Murat leaves.

Brian: (cont'd) Oh, God. I'm a wife. I'm a pathetic little tourist wife dying of diarrhea!

The call to prayer fades out. In the harem, Bedia follows Evelyn with towels. Her notebook in hand, Evelyn tries to get away from her.

Bedia: Hamam, hamam.

Evelyn: No, thank you , Bedia. I feel quite clean today.

Melek enters. Bedia leaves.

Melek: Evelyn? Aren't you going to join us in the bath?

Evelyn: No, thank-you. I think I will spend the morning in my room.

Melek: But you will be all alone.

Evelyn: I would like to be. I want to write.

Melek: But why? What would you write about? I don't understand why a woman would want to write when she can spend her time in the company of her friends.

Evelyn: How can you be happy like this Melek?

Melek: Don't you like it here?

Evelyn: I do. But you don't know what date it is. You don't even know what time of day it is. We never see a newspaper.

Melek: You can ask Papa what time it is, he would know. But today he's in Europe.

Evelyn: You never see men except through a lattice. Don't you see you're being kept prisoner in a gilded cage? The women in my country have demanded that they be given their rights. You have rights as well. But you must take action. You must demand them.

Melek: Are these the things you write about?

Evelyn: I've been writing about the harem and about you.

Ayshe enters.

Ayshe: Evelyn hanım için selâmlıkta ziyaretçi var, Melek.[19]

Melek: There is a visitor for you at the Selâmlık.

Evelyn exits. Kathy and Orhan on the boat.

---

[19] There is a visitor for Miss Evelyn in the selamlık.

Kathy: She would do it. I know she would. I can never get away from them, her and my mother. They're always controlling what I do.

Orhan: You mustn't be upset. We'll find a way.

Kathy: I know why I came here now. I wanted to get away from her. To get away from her sad, pathetic existence. I felt if I stayed with her I would turn out to be just like her.

Orhan: I think you came here for another reason. I think you came to find me.

Kathy: I don't believe in fate.

Orhan: Oh, but I do. You and I are meant for each other. We can do nothing to change that.

Wraps his arm around her, as though protecting her from the wind and the world.

Orhan: I want you to come with me to meet my family.

Kathy: What?

Orhan: Yes, it's time. If you meet my family your sister will be less worried. She'll know we're serious. Will you come with me tomorrow?

Evelyn enters the Selâmlık. Sir Robert Cave is waiting for her.

Sir Robert Cave: Good afternoon, Miss Crawley.

Evelyn: Good afternoon.

Sir Robert Cave: I'm Sir Robert Cave from the English Embassy. I'm sorry we haven't had the opportunity to meet on an earlier occasion. Things have been complicated, as you know. I hope you will forgive us.

Evelyn: I don't consider the embassy to have any obligation toward me.

Sir Robert Cave: But you're mistaken, Miss Crawley. We always make it our business to assure the well being of our countrymen in Constantinople. Especially in this time of war.

Evelyn: I understand.

Sir Robert Cave: Some concerns have been raised on the issue of your stay here in a Turkish house. It is our duty to ensure your safety.

Evelyn: I'm quite safe, thank-you.

Sir Robert Cave: Did you know that Vice Admiral Calthorpe is in Mudros to discuss the terms of an armistice?

Evelyn: No. I haven't seen a newspaper in some time.

Sir Robert Cave: You didn't know, then, that the master of this house is one of the plenipotentiaries who were summoned on board his Majesty's ships?

Evelyn: No.

Sir Robert Cave: Ah. Well, I'm pleased to tell you of our good news, then. An armistice has indeed been signed. The allied troops will enter the Dardanelles within two or three days.

Evelyn: Is Turkey to be occupied?

Sir Robert Cave: To be protected, more accurately. We must prevent its falling into a state of chaos.

Evelyn: To be protected...

Sir Robert Cave: In the face of such an eruptive situation, it is a matter of curiosity, Madam, why you have chosen such a peculiar residence. It is unusal for a British subject to live in a Turkish house.

Evelyn: Ali Riza Efendi's daughter is my friend. She invited me.

Sir Robert Cave: After all, Miss Crawley, we know that these are rather primitive people who do not understand our way of living. And I don't suppose you understand theirs. How do you feel about living in the house of a man with more than one wife? A house where concubines, not servants are employed, and where people use their fingers to feed themselves.

Evelyn: How long have you been in Constantinople, Sir Robert?

Sir Robert Cave: Nearly three years.

Evelyn: And in that period of time, have you made any effort to understand the culture of which you are here a guest? Have you visited a genuine Turkish home? Have you become acquainted with a Turkish man?

Sir Robert Cave: I've felt no need, Madam.

Evelyn: You stay at the Pera, in the midst of your countrymen, complaining how primitive a country this is and how barbaric its people. It is men like you who make me ashamed of being an Englishwoman, Sir. Your callowness and condescension are an embarrassment to my country. What do you know about the harem? Next to nothing, I assure you. Do not think I'm unaware of the Englishman's fascination with the harem. When the subject arises at our polite embassy parties, all the eyes of the men light up with curiosity. Wouldn't you like to have a house full of beautiful women ready to satisfy your every whim?

Sir Robert Cave: Miss Crawley, please control yourself!

Evelyn: Let me tell you something, Sir Robert. If I took you in there it would be an utter disappointment to you because it is entirely different from your childish, misinformed fantasy of it. A harem is a home just like any home.

Sir Robert Cave: I was going to spare you this, but there are rumors that are about to reach your father. Things you would not want English men to think of you, Madam. Or perhaps you would.... It is said that you have moved into this house to become another wife.

Evelyn: This meeting is concluded, Sir. I will return to my hotel at the Pera when I please.

Sir Robert Cave: I have brought you a recent edition of the London Times.

He gives it to her. She doesn't take it. He places it down on a chair.

Sir Robert Cave: (cont'd) The Turk has been on the strait for four and a half centuries. In all that time the country that he occupies has been exactly where it was when he arrived. The Turk has always stopped the clock of progress. And he has repressed progressive nations in order to do that.

We hear Melek's voice singing a sad song.

Sir Robert Cave: (cont'd) I sincerely hope, Madam, that you will read the newspaper that I brought you and that you will reconsider your unfortunate decision on this matter. Good day.

Cave exits. In the hotel room, Brian sits up in bed, looks at his watch.
He goes to the window and draws the curtains. The sun pours in. He
looks at his watch again. Worried, he goes to Murat's bag, opens it,
finds an address book and flips through it. He goes to the phone, lifts the
receiver and stands for a moment, in doubt. He dials a number.

Brian: Hello. I'm sorry, I hope you speak English. Oh, good.
May I speak to Sema Bayraktar, please. Hello, Miss
Bayraktar, my name is Brian. I'm a friend of your
brother's.

Melek sings. Blackout.

END OF ACT I

ACT II

Javid: (Speaks to the audience) Hello. My name's Javid.
Mademoiselle Crawley asked me to address you today. I
was raised as the son of a well-known and important
Pasha. I am, as are many others, the product of a
household in which there is more than one wife.I was a
happy child until the age of five when my father married
for the second time. The rest of my life passed in the bitter
and hopeless state of watching my poor mother suffer and
age over the years. The rooms of the wives were opposite
each other in the same hallway. At first my father visited
them in turn. On the nights when he went to the second
wife's room, my mother cried into her pillow until dawn.
Her anger and sadness eventually gave way to bitter
resignation, as, more and more, my father would choose to
go to the second wife's room. Not long after that, he
stopped knocking on my mother's door altogether. I was
so full of my mother's suffering and was so haunted by her
tear-stained, pale face, that all I could think about was to
leave that house forever and to never marry. She had
forever lost the one man she had ever loved and had been
displaced in her own home by a younger and more
beautiful woman. I pitied her but increasingly I became
angry with her. No woman of any dignity should be asked
to permit a second wife to enter her home. This practice
must change! But this change will not come about if you,
the women of this country, won't do something to change
it. (With disgust) I stand here looking at you in your veils
and I think you're despicable. Can't you see how Europe
laughs at you? Why do you put up with this iniquitous

situation? Why do you still wear those veils, the symbols of servitude? Why can't you come out and free yourselves? A veil is to keep you virtuous, say the hodjas. After five years of happiness, my mother remained virtuous but became utterly useless to anyone and completely alone.

Javid leaves. Osman and Bedia Older's house in 1952. Osman reads the newspaper. Bedia Older storms in followed by Javid Older and the maid, Ipek.

Bedia Older: Neden getiriyor bu kizi?[20] I'm a nervous wreck!

Javid Older: Bedia, Bedia, sakin ol Bedia.[21]

Bedia Older: Be calm, be calm. That's all you have to say. The girl is an American!

Javid Older: I know. You've said it a hundred times.

Bedia Older: He wouldn't humiliate the family. He wouldn't do that to us.

Javid Older: Only Allah can fathom what he would do.

Bedia Older: Infidels are dirty! They wash in still water like ducks. Splish splash. Don't you remember that wretch? What was her name?

Javid Older: Evelyn Crawley.

Bedia Older: Terrified of baths. She thought I was going to drown her. And they eat pork! Osman, say something! (Osman doesn't look up from his newspaper) They eat pork, Osman!

Javid Older: He hasn't talked to you in twenty years. Why should he start now?

---

[20] Why is she bringing this girl?
[21] Be calm, Bedia

Bedia Older: He's upset. Look at him, he's furious!

Javid Older: Yes. He's the picture of seething rage.

Bedia Older: (To Osman who is not listening) It's all because of that American school. (Fanning herself) Do you see what's happened, Osman, because you thought your children should be educated by the infidel?

Javid Older: Perhaps you should poke him. With your finger or a very sharp fork.

Bedia Older: (Slaps him with her fan) Osman, this is a crisis!

Osman: (Not looking up) What do you want me to do about it?

Javid Older: It's a miracle, it talks!

Bedia Older: Forbid it, of course!

Osman: How ridiculous!

Bedia Older: It's a doomed union! You must do it for the sake of your son.(The doorbell rings)Here they are. Allah have mercy on us. Osman, I want you to tell him you won't allow it and that will be that. He'll listen to you. Ipek! Don't just stand there like a broom, girl, open the door! (Osman begins to leave the room)Osman!

Osman's gone. Ipek opens the door. Orhan enters, followed by Kathy.

Orhan: Merhaba Anne'cigim.

Orhan kisses Bedia Older's hand and touches it to his forehead, according to custom. Motions toward Kathy.

Orhan: Bu Kathy.[22] Kathy, this is my Mother, Bedia hanim.

---

[22] This is Kathy

Bedia Older: (Extending her hand) Hoş geldiniz kizim.[23]

Kathy: (Shaking her hand. In shaky Turkish) Memnun oldum, Bedia hanim.[24]

Orhan: You are expected to kiss her hand, like I did. As an expression of respect.

Kathy does so.

Javid Older: Oh, don't make the poor girl...

Orhan: (Sarcastically) And this is our most unfortunate Javid.

Javid Older: I am not unfortunate, merely displaced. In place as well as in time. You're not obligated to kiss my hand, my dear.

Kathy: Memnun oldum, Javid .

Javid Older: Enchantée, ma fille. Aren't Turkish customs dreadful?

Orhan: You speak as though you yourself are not Turkish.

Javid Older: Of course I am. (To Kathy) But I'm a stubborn progressive. Many years I lived in Europe.

Orhan: Javid bey and my mother were raised in a konak together. He was the son of a pasha.

Javid Older: (To Kathy) Listen to him. He's saying it as though it's an insult. And my dear Bedia was.... well, never mind. I won't say it.

Orhan: She was a servant.

Javid Older: Yes. But a very good one.

---

[23] Welcome, my girl
[24] Nice to meet you, Bedia hanim

Orhan: Don't let him start telling you about his glorious childhood. You'll never hear the end of it.

Javid Older: Mais, Mademoiselle, vous êtes ravissante![25]

Orhan: And don't mind that, either. He still hasn't realized that everyone in the world does not speak French. Come to your senses, you old fool. The days of the dynasty are long over!

Javid Older: I may be an old fool, Orhan. But not foolish enough to think the world has been transformed forever, or that it won't be transformed again. You have no idea what the future may bring you, my boy.

Bedia Older: (Guiding Kathy to a chair) Otur, kizim.[26] Ipek!

Javid Older: I hope you will be comfortable in our intimate little chicken coop. We are dreadfully embarrassed to welcome guests here.

Bedia Older: Ipek, kahve getir.[27]

Osman re-enters. Orhan kisses his hand.

Orhan: Iyi günler, babacigim.[28](To Kathy) This is my Father, Osman Bey.

Kathy: (Kisses his hand) Memnun oldum, Osman Bey.

Osman: (Smiles) Bende memnun oldum.

Bedia Older: Can't she say anything other than, pleased to meet you, pleased to meet you? She's an idiot, this poor girl.

---

[25] You're ravishing Mademoiselle
[26] Sit down my girl.
[27] Ipek, bring coffee.
[28] Good day, father.

Orhan: She's learning some Turkish slowly.

Kathy: What is she saying? I think she hates me already.

Orhan: (Good naturedly) Nonsense! She adores you. Kathy Sabiha'nin hocasi.[29]

Bedia Older: Who cares. Look at her. She's pale as a sheet. She resembles a corpse. (Motioning with both hands upward to God) May Allah forgive us!

Kathy: What did you tell her?

Orhan: I said that you are Sabiha's teacher at Robert College. And she said, (Also motioning to God)...how wonderful!

Kathy: (To Bedia Older) Sabiha is a very good student.

Bedia Older: And look how skinny she is. I could just snap her bony legs like match-sticks.

Orhan: Mother, please.

Bedia Older: Osman, read your paper!

Ipek appears with a tray of coffee for everyone.

Bedia Older: (cont'd) Serve it to that skinny little thing over there, girl. Really, Orhan. She's just sitting there smiling at me like an invalid.

Orhan: Evleneceğim onunla.[30]

Javid Older gasps. Bedia Older springs to her feet, startling Ipek, who nearly drops her tray.

Bedia Older: Ne? Sen aklınımı kaçırdın?[31]

---

[29] Kathy is Sabiha's teacher
[30] I'm going to marry her.
[31] What? Have you lost your mind?

Orhan: Hayır Anne.[32]

Bedia Older: (Shrill) Sus, sus! Ağzını açma! Bir gâvurla evlenilirmi? Duyulmamış şey. Rezil, kepaze oluruz! Bütün Istanbul bize güler![33]

She marches out of the room. Orhan follows her. Osman pours drinks.

Javid Older: Bedia, please....

Orhan: Anne, Allahaşkına.[34]

Bedia Older: Konuşacak bir şey yok![35]

Bedia Older and Orhan exit. We hear Bedia Older shouting off-stage.

Bedia Older: (off) Kahrola Orhan! Aaaah! Ah! Ben seni bunun içinmi koynumda besledim. Bu ne nankörlük. Ne saygısızlık! Kalbimi kırdın Orhan! Çekil git gözümün önünden! [36]

Kathy: (Over the above) What's the matter? What are they fighting about?

Javid Older: Oh, they're not fighting. Just a discussion over mere trifles.

A big crash is heard off-stage.

Javid Older: Excuse me.

---

[32] No mother.
[33] Shut up, shut up! Don't open your mouth. Unheard of. We'll be humiliated. All of Istanbul will laugh at us.
[34] Mother for the love of Allah
[35] There's nothing to talk about
[36] Damn you Murat! AH! Did I nurse you in my arms so you would do this to me? You faithless child. What disrepect! You broke my heart, Orhan. Get away from me, get lost

Javid Older exits. Kathy is left alone with Osman. He's poured two drinks.

Osman: (Handing her the drink) Alırmısın?[37]

Kathy: What is it?

Osman: Rakı. Veri gud.

Kathy: (She takes it) Thank you.

Osman: (A toast) Şerefe.

Kathy: (She knows this word. They toast) Şerefe.

Osman: Veri gud?

Kathy: (Winces) Not really.

Osman: (Motions her to follow him) Gel, gel.[38]

Kathy: Where are we going?

Osman: Gel.

He leads her out to the balcony. Sound of traffic. Night sky.

Kathy: Oh, it's nice out here.

Osman: Büyük kepçe.

She looks up, not quite understanding what he means. He motions.

Osman: Küçük kepçe.

Kathy: Ah yes. Big dipper and small dipper.

Osman: (Motions) Kuzey yıldızı.

Kathy: Yes. North star.

Osman: Amerika aynımı?

---

[37] Will you have one?
[38] Come, come.

Kathy: What?

Osman: Amerika, Türkiye. Yıldızlar aynımı?

Kathy: Yes. It's the same sky in America.

Osman: (Smiles) Veri gud.

They drink. Both look at the sky.

In the hotel room there's a knock on the door. Kathy and Osman exit. Brian rushes out of the bathroom, pulling up his pants, almost tripping. He opens the door. It is Sema.

Brian: I wish you hadn't come. I told you over the phone...

Sema: May I come in?

Brian: (Letting her in. Struggling to hold up his pants) I was just a teensy bit worried about him. It's really nothing, really. I thought maybe he came to see you, but you told me he didn't, and that was fine. (Holds door open) Thanks for coming anyway. Bye now.

Sema: You said he disappeared. Does he disappear often?

Brian: Oh, yes, very frequently. He does it every day. Ordinary, ordinary circumstances. Nothing to worry about.

Sema: Why did you call me then?

Brian: I'm a silly, silly man, that's why. Sorry to have taken up your time. It's truly lovely to have met you. Bye bye.

Sema: I'm not leaving just yet.

Brian: Please, I beg you. He'll kill me. Have a heart, please.

Sema: How long has he been gone?

Brian: (Shuts the door reluctantly) Since early this morning.

He's going to be very upset if he sees you here.

Sema: Oh, you poor thing.

Brian: I beg your pardon?

Sema: (Laughing) I said, oh, you poor thing. What's the matter, can't understand my English?

Brian: I made a mistake. Please leave.

Sema: Let's see you try to make me.

Brian: Hello? Are you on crack? I'm asking you as politely as I can...

Sema: You're the one who called me... Brian.

Brian: I thought you might be... I don't know. A nicer person?

Sema: I don't have to be nice. He's my brother.

Brian: Please. Please.

Sema: (Beat) I'm sorry. I began our acquaintance on an unfortunate footing. Can you blame me, really, under the circumstances? I'm terribly upset.

Brian: There's no reason to be upset, he's fine. We're both fine. We're leaving in three days.

Sema: Why did he come?

Brian: *We.* We came together.

Sema: Whatever.

Brian: To see his family, I thought.

Sema: And as it turns out?

Brian: He's pretty confused. I've never seen him like this.

Sema: Then we must help him, mustn't we?

Brian: I don't think there's anything left that I can do, short of shoving half a bottle of valium and depositing him at their door. You wouldn't happen to have any on you, would you?

Sema: Not exactly valium, but the Turkish version. Probably stronger. Turks like their medicine strong. Would you like one?

Brian: I really shouldn't.

Sema takes bottle out of her purse. Gives him one.

Sema: Here. Just one never hurt anyone.

Brian takes the pill, comtemplates.

Sema: Addiction problem?

Brian: No. I mean yes. Small.

Sema: Wonderful! See, we're already finding things in common.

Brian: (He pops the pill and swallows) God, that feels good.

Sema: I know. Are we friends now?

Brian: Excuse me. Have we met?

Sema: I predict we'll be the best of friends in about twenty-three and a half minutes.

Brian: What do you want?

Sema: I want to sit here and wait for him to arrive and have a nice chat with you, in the interim.

Brian: Sorry, I can't. I have a mandatory date with the toilet today.

Sema: Ah, Turkish tummy. Don't worry. It'll be gone in about three weeks.

Brian: (From the bathroom door) Three weeks?

Sema: Just kidding.

Brian: Can I just say something? I think it's barbaric to eat intestines. Or anything digestive like that.

Sema: Try balls.

Brian: I'm sorry?

Sema: Testicles. Grilled. Ram's eggs, they're called. One of Murat's favorites. I'm surprised he hasn't gotten them for you.

Brian: Man, this has been a hell of a vacation.

Sema: Yes. And if you stick around, no doubt it will only improve.

Brian shuts the bathroom door. At the house Kathy comes on followed by Osman. Kathy is finishing her drink.

Kathy: (Wincing) I have to say, this is the vilest thing I've ever tasted. May I have another please?

Osman: Veri gud?

Kathy: Yes. Veri gud.

Javid Older enters.

Javid Older: Mes felicitations, Mademoiselle! (Kisses Kathy on both cheeks) I'm very happy for both of you.

Kathy: For what?

Javid Older: For your engagement, of course!

Kathy: Engagement?

Javid Older: An American bride. A dream come true! We're thrilled.

Kathy: What on earth are you...?

Javid Older: (Motioning toward Osman) Just go over there and kiss his hand, my dear. I know it's dreadful but it is expected of every new bride.

Kathy: I'm not kissing anyone's hand. He didn't even propose!

Javid Older: But that's only a technicality, isn't it?

Kathy: No it isn't. I haven't consented to marry him.

Javid Older: Ah. Shame. Turkish men don't concern themselves with such sentiments. What really matters is your heart, Mademoiselle.

Kathy: (Putting on her coat) Is that what all the yelling is about? Because he told her that?

Javid Older: It's nothing, darling. Marriages always cause havoc in Turkish homes. It is our custom.

Kathy: There is to be no marriage! You people are all out of your minds.

Kathy leaves, slams the door.

Osman: Ne oluyor Allahaşkına?[39]

Javid Older: She's our bride! Isn't she stunning?

Evelyn's room at the harem. Evelyn is writing. Melek enters, excited.

Melek: Evelyn, did you hear the wonderful news? The war is over! An armistice was signed and the war is finally over

---

[39] What's happening for the love of Allah?

and Papa is coming home! He'll arrive in two days. No more shortages, no more wounded soldiers. I'm so happy, I could fly!

Evelyn: That's wonderful, Melek.

Melek: (Giggles) And I did something terrible. You won't guess what it is. I bribed Refik Aga again and he took me to the house of Ali Shevket Efendi, my future husband. And we watched the house for two hours and Ali Shevket Efendi finally came out and I saw him! Isn't that insane? I can't believe I did such a thing.

Evelyn: What does he look like?

Melek: He's young! Barely in his thirties and very handsome. He's so wonderful Evelyn, I'm in love.

Evelyn: I'm very happy for you, Melek.

Melek: Will you please come to the salon and celebrate?

Evelyn: Of course.

Melek: Except don't tell the others what I did. If Papa finds out he will never speak to me again.

Evelyn and Melek exit. Orhan and Bedia Older enter. Osman quickly puts up the paper again.

Bedia Older: This is an outrage! I'm telling you for the last time: she's not welcome in our family!

Orhan: You're not listening, Mother. This is my decision.

Bedia Older: Unheard of! Impossible! The mother always selects an appropriate bride for her son. Have you eaten your brain with bread and cheese?

Orhan: Where's Kathy?

Javid Older: She left!

Bedia Older: Good riddance! See how rude she is? She didn't even say good-bye!

Orhan: Why? Why did she leave?

Bedia Older: What do you expect from a Christian? No manners! She doesn't know our customs. She wasn't raised properly. She speaks another language. And what about religion? Is she willing to convert?

Orhan: We haven't discussed that yet.

Bedia Older: Hah! She'll never do it!

Javid Older: Look! It's her coffee cup. Ipek, come here at once. Make yourself useful.

Ipek takes the coffee cup and sits on the floor

Bedia Older: Osman, are you listening to this? And what about her parents? Who are they? Where do they live? Are they well known in America?

Orhan: Her family lives in a place called Ohio.

Bedia Older: What is this Ohio? Is it a city? Is it a village? Where is it?

Orhan: I believe it's in the area they call the middle west. Somewhere in the middle of the country, I suppose.

Bedia Older: Wonderful! It's not even a city, it's a village. These people are peasants. Where is my kolonya? My heart is going to stop!

Javid Older: (Holding her up. To Orhan) Tell her about the family, tell her how important the father is.

Orhan: Yes, yes. Her family is very well known. Her father is the... the Minister of the Interior!

Javid Older: My word! How impressive.

Bedia Older: Of America?

Orhan: Yes!

Bedia Older: So what, who cares? Osman, are you listening to this?

Osman grunts, turns away

Bedia Older: Don't you have anything to say? Do you give your consent to this charade?

Osman: Yes, I do, yes. May I read the paper now?

Bedia Older: He says yes. He doesn't even know what we're talking about...Your father gave his consent. Are you happy now?

Orhan: I want your consent too.

Ipek: (Looking inside Kathy's coffee cup) Do you see here, how the girl's head is coming out of the water? It means she's about to come to an important decision. A happy decision that will open up her heart to heaven. And look. Look over here.

Bedia Older: What are they?

Ipek: They're deer. Baby deer. It means she's going to bear five beautiful children. And her husband's going to be very wealthy and a good provider. I see a happy family here, a bright future.

Orhan: She's a nice girl. She'll respect and obey you. She'll learn the language. She can already speak a few words...

Bedia Older: (Interrupting) I know, I know. "Nice to meet you, nice to meet you." She's memorized it like a parrot. Can she go to the market? Can she buy eggs and okra?

Javid Older: Inhale it, Bedia. There, now. Isn't that nice? Now tell Orhan how happy you are that he is getting married.

Bedia Older: I suppose we should decide on a date for the wedding.

Orhan: (Hugging her) Thank you Mother. You're the best mother in the world. I promise, she will make you proud.

Bedia Older: Go away, go away. I have many things to think about.

Orhan: I'll go and tell her the good news right away.

Orhan leaves

Bedia Older: I must get on the phone and reserve the ballroom at the club. Javid, you make a list of people to invite.

Javid Older: Yes, yes, certainly.

Bedia Older: At least two hundred people must be invited. No, three hundred. (To Osman) I'm going to spend all your money. The minister of the interior of America. (Chuckles) People will be green with envy.

At the hotel room, Brian comes out of the bathroom. Sema is there.

Brian: I love this pill. I'm going to have to get me some of this pill.

Sema: (Looking out) Do you like our city?

Brian: I'm inspired by your city. I'm flooded with ideas for my work.

Sema: Are you in the design business?

Brian: Yeah.

Sema: Architecture?

Brian: No. (Beat) Tiles.

Sema: Tiles?

Brian: Yeah, I design custom tiles for yuppies, okay? Yuppy tiles for yuppy bathrooms and yuppy kitchens.... Somehow I knew you'd find that amusing.

Sema: It's amusing that one can make a living doing that sort of thing.

Brian: Honey, you'd be surprised.

Sema: And Murat. Is he a success?

Brian: He's brilliant. And very much in demand.

Sema: I take it you're living together and you are... You and Murat, I mean...

Brian: (Fingers) We're "lovers," yes.

Sema: What is the meaning of that gesture?

Brian: Man! It's a quote. I'm sorry. It's a bad habit.

Sema: Yes, it is bad. And how long have you been (fingers) "lovers?"

Brian: Nearly eight years. He hasn't told you?

Sema: No. (Pause) I'll step outside for a moment, if it's alright with you.

Brian: Sure. Feel free to take a little jump. It's only five stories.

Sema goes out to the balcony. She begins to cry. Brian steps outside after a few moments.

Brian: Hey, I was just kidding...

Sema: I don't know what I thought. That he didn't have a life? Of course he would have a lover. Of course he would have him for eight years. Of course he wouldn't tell me. He's my brother and I miss him and I don't know anything about his life. Is he happy, is he in good health, nothing. Miserable!

Brian: Sweetheart, that's why the man is here.

Sema: (She wipes her eyes) Can you leave me alone for a moment? I don't know what's come over me. I'm usually not sentimental.

Brian steps inside. Suddenly he hears Murat inserting his key in the lock. Brian runs for the bathroom. Murat enters. Brian sticks his head out.

Brian: Hi, sweetie-pie! How was your day?

Murat: Fine. What kinds of tips are you handing out anyway?

Brian: Me? Tips?

Murat: Yeah, you, tips. I'm being treated like royalty everywhere in this building. You look like you're feeling better.

Brian: Absolutely not! I haven't left the bathroom in hours. And guess what. We're out of toilet paper. You'll have to go downstairs.

Murat: I'll call the front desk.

Brian: No! It'll take too long.

Murat: They'll have an extravaganza celebration.

Brian: I need the stuff like yesterday.

Murat: Call it the American Queen's tissue festival.

Sema enters from balcony

Sema: Merhaba, Murat.

Brian: Who is that? I don't even know who that is!

Quickly shuts the door

Murat: (Turns to her)Sema? My God... How did you...

Sema: A little bird told me.

Murat: (Calling, his eyes on Sema) Brian, come out here!

Sema: (Smiling) Don't be mad at him. He was terribly worried.

Murat: Brian, I'm calling you!

Brian: (From the bathroom. Affecting voice like telephone operator) We're sorry. Your call cannot be connected as dialed. Please hang up and try again later. Click.

Sema: (Laughs) He's sweet.

Murat: (Smiles in spite of himself) He's terrible.

Sema: Don't I deserve a hug?

Murat: (Going to her) Yes. God, yes.

The two fall into each other's arms. Sema sobs hard.

Sema: I'm sorry. I don't think I've cried since I was five. I'd forgotten what a nasty business it is.

Murat: It's alright.

Sema: Stand back. Let me look at you. (Murat does) You look good. You've gained weight.

Murat: You haven't changed.

Sema: (Laughs) I rather wish I had.

Murat: I'm glad he called. I didn't have the guts... How is Ali?

Sema: Oh, fine.

Murat: Still the big secret?

Sema: Definitely.

Murat: I don't know how you do it.

Sema: It's easier than you think.

Murat: How are Mom and Dad?

Sema: My, this day is filled with difficult questions. I would venture to say that they're fine. At least they think they're fine although opinions differ.

Murat: How do *you* think they are.

Sema: Mother is in a sort of perpetual daze, like someone who sits all day watching the ships sail by. She's devoted to her charity work, to staying out of the way of gossip, and her most recent interest, knitting sweaters that don't fit anyone. She's become rather a rock. Does that say very much?

Murat: And Dad?

Sema: Where shall I start?

Murat: Is he drinking?

Sema: Oh, yes. An amount he himself has deemed reasonable. He still calls it social drinking but it's not social anymore since he drinks mostly by himself. If you're in the room, he will certainly attempt to indulge you but he does occasionally accept defeat. He's almost always irrational and angry. Never fails to make a scene wherever he goes. Every maitre d' in the city cringes when he walks through the door. He's not a rock at all, he's a spewing volcano. He misses you terribly. They both do.

Murat: I would like to see them. Should I?

Sema: (Pause. Slowly) What for, Murat?

Murat: Just to see them. I miss them too.

Sema: His health isn't good. He smokes nearly three packs a day, doesn't brush his teeth, never got in the habit he says, and he's rather proud of that. His teeth have all rotted to the bone but of course he refuses to see a dentist or any doctor of any kind. He's overweight...

Murat: (Interrupting) Why aren't you answering my question?

Sema: (Continuing) The boil on his ass, which he calls a cyst, and it isn't a cyst at all...

Murat: Why won't you tell me? What are you trying to say?

Sema: (Her anger rising) ...it's just a big, nasty infection that has snugly embedded itself so deep into his body over the years that...

Murat: Sema, please...

Sema: ...that it has grown arms like an octopus! It continually causes him pain and he has to clean it out two or three times a day...

Murat: Sema, stop.

Sema: ...BECAUSE OTHERWISE THE PUSS, THE

BLOOD, WHATEVER THE HELL IT IS, OOZES
OUT THROUGH HIS PANTS AND....

Murat: STOP!

Brian enters.

Sema: WHAT IS IT WITH YOU? WHAT DO YOU
WANT FROM THEM? (Beat) You've made of yourself a
huge spectacle, Murat, isn't it enough? You broke their
hearts, they grieve every day, isn't it enough? Have you
come back for more? What have they left to give to you?

Murat: You don't mean this. You can't possibly mean this!

Sema: But I do! What do you want here? Why have you
come?

Murat: This is my home!

Sema: You've made your choices, you've done something
else with your life. This family *cannot* follow you through
your every whim. This country cannot follow you. You
don't have a home here anymore. Go back and leave them
alone because they can't, they can't handle it, do you
understand, they never could and they never will. All you
will do is cause them more pain and cause yourself more
pain. It's not worth it, don't you see?

Murat: I worry about her all the time. Him too, but mostly
her.

Sema: She too has made her choices. You can't just ride up
on your horse and rescue her from herself like a valiant
knight. She doesn't want you to.

Pause. Calmly now, but hurting.

Sema: I'm sorry I'm so harsh. But you could not have

expected me to feel differently. We tried to protect them all our lives, you and I, and that's all I'm trying to do now. I know you understand that.

Murat: Yes.

Sema: Shit. I have to be in court in fifteen minutes. I have to go...I'll call you tomorrow. Maybe we can go out to dinner.

Murat: Sure.

They hug. Sema goes to the door.

Sema: (Turns back) Oh. I almost forgot.

She takes the bottle of pills out of her purse. Hands it to Brian.

Sema: I want you have these.

Brian: No. Really, I can't.

Sema: Please. I have a trunkful at home.

Brian: (Taking them) Well, in that case...

Murat: What are they?

Sema: Nothing. Just our little secret.

Sema leaves.

Murat: What are they, Brian?

Brian: Nothing. I just had a headache and...

Murat: Hand them over. (Brian hesitates) Please...

Brian hands him the pills. Murat looks at them.

Murat: Why?

Kathy is there. Orhan enters.

Orhan: Kathy?

Kathy doesn't answer.

Orhan: Kathy, why did you leave?

Kathy: Go away. I don't want to see you.

Orhan: Why?

Kathy: How could you? HOW COULD YOU DO THAT TO ME?

Orhan: What? What have I done?

Kathy: How could you tell her we were getting married without even bothering to tell me?

Orhan: I'm sorry. I only assumed...

Kathy: Don't assume, Orhan! You're not allowed to make any assumptions about me. I left home because I was SICK of people making assumptions about me. I make my own decisions and I have *not* decided to marry you.

Orhan: You won't marry me?

Kathy: You haven't even asked!

Orhan: Then I'm asking you now. You can't leave me. I'm so in love with you Kathy, that I couldn't live without you.

Kathy: Love! How can two people like us build a life together? Did you ever think about that?

Orhan: What would be in our way?

Kathy: Your mother would be in our way. An entire country would be in our way.

Orhan: My mother's not very bright. She thinks with her heart instead of her brain. Once you say yes to me, she'll love you like her own.

Kathy: I don't know if I can adapt. There's so much I don't understand.

Orhan: You don't have to adapt. You'll be yourself. Turkish women need to see a woman like you. You'll be an example to them.

Kathy: And what about our children? What will they be like? Will they be happy? Will they be normal? And what about religion? Will love answer all these questions?

Orhan: My mother was given away by her family to go live in a rich man's home. She was raised as a concubine, Kathy, a slave. And even after slavery was abolished, she did not want her freedom because she was afraid of change. She was forced to marry a man she hadn't met and whom she did not love. Look at me, Kathy. (She does) My life won't be whole without you. We have a future together. I know you feel this too.

Kathy: I don't know if I should feel it, Orhan. I don't know if it's right.

Orhan: I'm not perfect. But I'm not afraid of change. I know you want to say yes. Will you marry me, Kathy? Will you please say yes to me, now?

Kathy: Yes.

Orhan: (Holds her tight) Yes!

Kathy: YES! YES! A HUNDRED TIMES, A MILLION TIMES YES!

Orhan kisses her passionately. Ali Riza Efendi enters at the harem.

Ali Riza Efendi: Hello, my little robin!

Melek: (Running to him) Papa! I'm so glad you're home.

Ali Riza Efendi: I have great news. A wedding date has been set for you. The first day of April!

Melek: I'm so happy, I can fly!

Ali Riza Efendi: (Sees Evelyn) Mademoiselle Crawley! How nice to see you.

Evelyn: I wish I could say the same, Ali Rıza Efendi.

Ali Riza Efendi: I beg your pardon.

Evelyn: I'm dreadfully disappointed that you're doing this to your daugher. Have you no love for her? Have you no concern?

Melek: Papa loves me, Evelyn!

Ali Riza Efendi: There is no one in the world that I love more than Melek, Mademoiselle. But how can I prevent it? Do you think I want her to get married? I will not see her anymore, I will lose her forever.

Melek: I want to get married. I want to, Papa, I'm happy to.

Evelyn: You are an educated, worldly man and you still treat your women exactly the same despicable way Europe, and particularly England, treats your country. As a commodity. Something to be bought and used for your own selfish purposes.

Ali Riza Efendi: England has nothing but our best interests in mind.

Evelyn: Then why has she made you sign your country's death warrant? You are naïve, Ali Rıza Efendi. The armistice was signed by a single English official in the name of the allies. They have divided Turkey amongst themselves. And you have put your signature on that obscene document!

Ali Riza Efendi: It is unfortunate that you feel this way. I have only done what I believe is the best for my country, what the Sultan believes.

Evelyn: Your Sultan, Monsieur, has become a puppet in the hands of foreigners.

Ali Riza Efendi: That's enough! I assume you know that I am much too polite to ask you to leave my house.

Evelyn: I will leave of my own accord, Monsieur.

Ali Riza Efendi: Yes. I think it would be for the best.

Ali Riza Efendi exits.

Melek: Why did you do this, Evelyn? You are my dear friend. You have tried to teach me to become a woman like you. But I don't want to, don't you see? I am not interested in a career or my abilities or my independence. I'm not interested in being a woman like you who thinks of herself more than she does of her friend. So put me in your book. But put me as a woman who is proud of who she is and proud of her country. A woman who disagrees with your way of life.

Evelyn: I'm sorry, Melek. I simply cannot accept that. You are not a woman. You're only a girl.

Evelyn leaves. At the hotel, Murat dials the phone.

Murat: Hello, Mother?... Hi... Yes, it's me, Murat... How are you?... I'm here, Mom. I'm in Istanbul, at the Pera Palas Hotel. Yes. Really. No, I'm not joking. I'm...(Looks at Brian) ...we're here.

At the harem, Melek talks to Neyime.

Melek: Are you happy, Neyime? Are you happy with your life?

Neyime: It doesn't matter, my precious.

Melek: But it does matter. It does. Are you as sad as Javid says?

Neyime: Look outside, my dear. All the allied ships have entered the Bosphorus. There must be a hundred of them. And look across. Do you see all the Christians? They are rejoicing. But why? What have we done to them? We have lived with them for centuries as friends and neighbors. Why do they hate us so?

At the hotel, Murat hangs up the phone.

Brian: Come here, sweetheart.

Murat goes to him. Brian kisses Murat.

Brian: You did the right thing.

Murat: Tomorrow. They're expecting us.

Brian: Man, I didn't think I'd be nervous but I'm shaking. What will they think of me? What should I be for them? How should I appear?

Murat: They'd love it if you were an American chick with big tits and blonde all over.

Brian: I can do that. I can do that very well.

Murat: Just be yourself. Please, always be yourself.

Evelyn speaks to the audience.

Evelyn: And now the time has come for me to return to England, where, drudging through traffic and government offices all run by men, I'll have to prove my worth at every turn. Had not circumstances forced me to work out my own destiny, I should perhaps not quarrel with what is part of a Turkish woman's existence. It is tempting to run back to the harem and join again my sweet, innocent Melek, watch the sunrise with her over the Bosphorus and walk in our lovely garden, concerned with nothing but the smell of roses. Always protected from the world, with no responsibilities or ambitions, only kept as delicate ornaments. It is everything I love about this country and at the same time everything I despise. How sad it is that part of the charm of this land is exactly what will have to change. Like death, the passing of the old Turk is inevitable. But the absolute sincerity of the east, the liking of one's friends for friendship's sake, the democracy of the kindly Turk, if these qualities must vanish in the inevitable march of progress, then it would no longer be the Turkey that I have admired and loved.

END OF ACT II

ACT III

The home of Kathy Older and Orhan Older. Orhan Older enters through the front door, out of breath. He sits down heavily and lights a cigarette. Kathy Older enters.

Kathy Older: Hello, Orhan. How did everything go?

Orhan Older: Terrible. Don't ask. I'm in a coma. They're taking me to court!

Kathy Older: You're not serious!

Orhan Older: Surprised? Not me! You waste away your life, trying to do honest business in this country, while left and right people are cheating each other and cheating the government and I'm the one that gets thrown in jail! Me! The only honest, hard working man around.

Kathy Older: You're not going to jail, Orhan.

Orhan Older: Sure, you know everything, Kathy. They're asking three to five years, what do you say to that? Now, where are my slippers?

Kathy Older: I have something to tell you.

Orhan Older: Goddamnit, this woman hides everything. Why do we keep her?

Kathy Older: I have something to tell you, Orhan.

Orhan Older: She can't do anything right. I've told you a hundred times. Fire the prune!

Kathy Older: Orhan listen to me!

Orhan Older: What? I can't find my slippers!

Kathy Older: Murat is here.

Orhan Older: (A moment. He's not sure he's heard right) What?

Kathy Older: I said Murat is here.

Orhan Older: Here where?

Kathy Older: In Istanbul. At the Pera Palas Hotel.

Orhan Older: Why? What is he doing there?

Kathy Older: I don't know. I don't know. He called and he said I'm here and I don't know. I don't know if I should be happy or angry or worried.

Orhan Older: Is he alright? Is he in trouble?

Kathy Older: He sounded perfectly fine. Like he spoke to me yesterday.

Orhan Older: Why isn't he here at home?

Kathy Older: I don't know.

Orhan Older: Didn't you ask him, Kathy?

Kathy Older: I was in shock!

Orhan Older: What do you mean you were in shock? He's your son, for God's sake!

Kathy Older: (Over) I was in shock, I was in shock!

Orhan Older: That's stupid, Kathy. There's no reason to be in shock. I'll go over there right now.

Kathy Older: No. Don't.

Orhan Older: Why not? Why the hell not? What's the matter with you?

Kathy Older: He's with a friend.

Orhan Older: So?

Kathy Older: I think you should leave them alone. They're coming over tomorrow.

Orhan Older: You didn't tell them to come over tonight?

Kathy Older: I didn't know what to say.

Orhan Older: What kind of a stupid thing is that?

Kathy Older: (Crying) I'm sorry. I didn't know how you'd feel.

Orhan Older: How *I* would feel? I would feel fine. He's my son. He should be here, where he belongs and he should bring his friend. You didn't know how I'd feel. That's nonsense. And stop sniveling. There's no reason to get all emotional. I'm going to jail and I have to deal with your tears?

Kathy Older: You're not going to jail! Don't say that!

Orhan Older: Look, Kathy. Whatever happened between me and Murat ten years ago...

Kathy Older: Nine years ago!

Orhan Older: ...whatever, is over, finished. We have completely forgotten the past. The past is not an issue.

Kathy Older: That's not possible. It doesn't work that way.

Orhan Older: ...I'm going to go call him right now and...

Kathy Older: Don't. They're coming over tomorrow. Maybe

they want some privacy.

Orhan Older: No, Kathy. They're coming over tonight. Now please make me a drink.

Kathy Older: I just don't want anything bad to happen. I don't want you people fighting each other.

Orhan Older: (Going to the phone) And don't let the stupid prune make it. She can't make a drink, she can't make anything, that stupid prune.

The hotel room. There is a knock on the door. Evelyn goes to answer it. It is Javid.

Evelyn: Javid! What a surprise! Come in.

Javid: Bonjour, Mademoiselle Crawley.

Evelyn: Bonjour, mon ami. It's been a long time. Almost four years.

Javid: I heard you were in Istanbul and I had to come see you and ask how you are.

Evelyn: I'm well, thank you. I've just returned from Ankara.

Javid: Ankara? Really?

Evelyn: I was invited by Mustafa Kemal. I was the only foreign journalist in the area. Rather thrilling, really.

Javid: But isn't it dangerous for a woman? And how did you get there? We've heard the railways are cut off at all the junctures.

Evelyn: On foot and bullock carts. It was quite an adventure.

Orhan Older: (Looking up the number) He's in Istanbul and he took a room in a hotel. He didn't even tell us he was coming. How do you explain that?

Kathy Older: (Entering with his drink) I can't explain it.

Orhan Older: You should know. Mothers have a kind of intuition or something.

Kathy Older: Mothers have nothing of the kind.

Javid: Is it true that he intends to take Constantinople?

Orhan Older: (On phone) Hello, Pera Palas? Get me Murat Bayraktar's room, please.

Evelyn: What?

Javid: The Sultan thinks Mustafa Kemal wants to take Istanbul and abolish the Sultanate. Papa is worried. He cannot believe that all of us, including the Sultan, invested our trust in him at one time.

Evelyn: Mustafa Kemal is a great man, Javid. He wants to establish a modern, democratic republic. He invited me to hear my thoughts on the position of women in Turkey. He feels a democracy cannot exist if half the country is in bondage.

Orhan Older: (Hangs up) They're out. How do you like that? Are you proud of what you've done?

Javid: Do you like him then?

Evelyn: Yes. I've never met anyone like him and I think he's a remarkable man. (Beat) When I last saw you, Javid, you were a sad boy. Now you're a grown man and you still seem so sad. How is Melek?

Javid: She's the real reason I came.

Evelyn: What is it?

Javid: We haven't seen Melek since she married. She's not allowed to leave her husband's house or to have any visitors. Recently Bedia heard that she is sad and she cries all the time.

Evelyn: But this is barbaric Javid. Your father should not allow it.

Javid: I came to ask you to go see her for me, Mademoiselle Crawley. You are English and they will do what you ask. Will you do that for me, please?

Kathy and Anne enter the hotel room with packages.

Anne: And what about the blue scarf?

Kathy: Give that to Lisa. She would like that. And the prayer rug to Aunt Lois and the ivory chess set to uncle Dave. I hope I'm not forgetting anyone.

Anne: You astound me. What a bargainer you've become.

Kathy: I'm a Turkish woman now.

Anne: Are you happy, Kathy?

Kathy: Yes. I'm happy.

Anne: Then why are you crying?

Kathy: Because I hate for you to leave.

Anne: You knew it had to happen sooner or later.

Kathy: I know. But we've never been apart.

Anne: You don't think you...

Kathy: What?

Anne: Made a mistake, do you?

Kathy: Of course not. I love my husband.

Anne: But living with your in laws...

Kathy: I don't mind. My mother-in-law is wonderful. She teaches me everything.

Anne: You have a family here. It's your family.

Kathy: Yes. It's a good family.

Anne: Come on. Dry your tears before Orhan comes and sees you upset.

Murat's getting ready. Brian enters wearing a tie.

Murat: You packed a tie? You look like you're going to church.

Brian: Same difference. Meeting my in-laws.

Murat: They're not your in-laws. In-laws come to your wedding. They bring a dishwasher or a porche.

Brian: You're so materialistic, Murat. All you think about are things.

Murat: Please. Take it off.

Brian: I'll make you proud, my pet. You just watch. (Sprays breath freshener) Ready.

Murat: Oh, Mary!

Orhan enters. Murat and Brian leave.

Orhan: Hello, ladies.

Kathy: (Goes to kiss him) Hello, dear. How did it go?

Orhan: (He gives her a twirl) I think it went very well. I believe they will hire me.

Kathy: Wonderful! I'm so proud of you.

Orhan: (To Anne) I applied for a position in Joe's firm. Did Kathy tell you?

Anne: Yes. That's terrific, Orhan. They'll be thrilled to have someone like you.

Orhan: It means we'll have to move to Ankara, but that would be alright for a few years. Of course we hate to see you leave.

Anne: Yes. In less than a week.

Orhan: Why don't you come over for dinner tomorrow night. Kathy, have you asked your sister?

Kathy: Yes, Anne, why not?

Anne: Joe's coming tomorrow...

Orhan: Wonderful! We'll all be together like a happy family.

Kathy: (Over. Clapping hands and jumping) Yey!

The living room of Kathy Older and Orhan Older. The doorbell. Orhan Older rushes to answer it. Murat and Brian enter.

Orhan Older: Well, well, well! Welcome home, you big rascal! Come give your old father a kiss. Kathy, they're here!

Murat kisses his father. Kathy Older rushes in. Everything from now on is at a nervous, frantic pace.

Kathy Older: Hello, hello! We're so glad you're here, my darling. We're so happy to see you.

Murat: I'm happy to see you too. I'm sorry.

Kathy Older: For what, my darling?

Murat: No, I'm not. I'm not sorry.

Orhan Older: He didn't tell us he was coming.

Kathy Older: (Mock scolding) Ohh... Naughty, naughty.

Orhan Older: That's what he's sorry about, you naughty boy, you.

Kathy Older: It's alright, Orhan. The important thing is that he's here.

Murat: This is Brian.

Brian: Hello.

Orhan Older: (over) Of course, of course, Brian. Sema told us about you.

Brian: I was afraid of that. Nothing "good," I suspect.

Orhan Older: Oh, no...

Kathy Older: (over) Oh, yes...

Orhan Older: (over) Only good things. She said you're a very nice young man...

Kathy Older: (over) Of course...

Orhan Older: (over) ...and that you're concerned with Murat's well being which is great news for us because...

Kathy Older: (over) ...yes...

Orhan Older: (over) ...you see, we don't see our son often anymore and probably he won't believe this but we love him and we miss him and we want to know how he's doing.

Kathy Older: Yes, very much.

Murat: I believe you.

Orhan Older: (Going to the living room. Others follow him) You don't have to believe me, Murat. You can believe anything that you want.

Murat: But, I believe you.

Kathy Older: He does, Orhan.

Orhan Older: No matter, it's not important. (To Brian) The important thing is that he has someone like you in his life who cares about him. This gives me great comfort inside and I will tell you right now... (open arms) ...that I love you. (kisses Brian on both cheeks) And that you are welcome in our home.

Kathy Older: (genuinely moved) Ahhhh. Isn't that just...

Brian: (rather stunned) Thanks.

Orhan Older: Now sit! Relax! Can I fix you a drink?

Brian: No, thanks.

Kathy Older: (with tray) Would you like an hors-d'oeuvre?

Brian: No. I won't be eating again until we're back in America.

Orhan Older: Nonsense! Your mother's prepared a delicious dinner.

Kathy Older: Wonderful! Murat, would you like an hors-d'oeuvre?

Orhan Older: And Sema will be here in a minute and we'll all be happy together again as a family. Isn't that wonderful?

Kathy Older: Wonderful, wonderful.

Murat: Great.

Brian: That's wonderful.

Kathy Older: (To Brian) Are you sure you won't have an hors-d'oeuvre?

Kiraz, the maid enters and rushes straight to Murat. She's a small, exuberant woman. She coos, kisses and pinches his cheeks and speaks a mile minute in Turkish throughout the following while the rest talk over her.

Kiraz: Aman Yarabbim, şu güzel çocuğa bir bak! Ne de büyümüş, kocaman olmuş benim güzel oğlum! Hem de ne boy! Hoş geldin çocugum. Çok memnun olduk. Anan seni nasıl özledi, evladım. Benim yakışıklı çocugum.[40]

Orhan Older: Oh, for heaven's sake...

Kathy Older: This is Kiraz, our maid. She's a real character.

Orhan Older: She's an ignorant peasant.

Murat: Merhaba, Kiraz hanım.

She squeezes Kathy Older's cheeks, all the while chirping.

Kiraz: Yanakların nasıl kızarmış, hanımefendi, ne memnunsun, değilmi?[41]

Kathy Older: Her name means cherry but my husband calls her prune.

Orhan Older: Ech! She's terrible with housework. Can't cook a thing.

Kathy Older: To her face! Prune! Just like that.

---

[40] My goodness, look at this beautiful boy! How he grew, got so big, my boy. And what height! Welcome my child. We're so happy. Your mother's so happy.

[41] Your cheeks are flushed, you're so happy my lady.

Kiraz goes to Brian and squeezes and hugs him as well.

Kiraz: Aman buda kim? Buda başka bir yakışıklı. Gel oğlum senide öpeyim.[42]

Orhan Older: All she does is run around hugging people.

Kathy Older: She loves us. She adores all of us.

Orhan Older: She's become part of the family! Unheard of! (To Kiraz) Hadi muşmula, git işine![43]

This strikes Kiraz to be extremely funny. She bursts into laughter.

Kiraz: Ah, ne komiksiniz, beyefendi! Bana muşmula diyor, gördünüzmü? Çok tatlısınız vallahi, vallahi.[44]

Murat: (Half laughing, overlaps with Kiraz above) Don't say that to her face.

Kathy Older: (To Brian, also overlapping with Kiraz) There, you see? Prune. to her face.

Kiraz: (Patting Orhan Older's cheek) Çok komik, çok komik.[45]

Sema enters through the front door with a package.

Sema: Hello, everyone!

Orhan Older: There she is!

Kathy Older: Hello, Sema!

Kiraz immediately goes to her and kisses her on both cheeks, twittering excitedly. Sema hands her the package of dessert.

---

[42] And who is this? Another handsome one. Come my boy, let me kiss you too.
[43] Go to your work, you prune.
[44] Oh, you're so funny, sir! Look, he called me a prune. You're so sweet. Very funny. Very funny.
[45] Very funny, Very funny.

Kiraz: Hoş geldin, güzelim. Ayol her gelişinde bir daha güzel oluyorsun. Ne getirdin bakayım? Yaşa evladım. Her gelişinde bir şey getirir. Hiç unutmaz.[46]

Orhan Older: Don't mind the peasant! Come in!

Kiraz exits

Orhan Older: Sema, have you heard? I'm going to jail!

Sema: You're not going to jail, Father.

Kathy Older: Really, Orhan...

Murat: What are you talking about?

Orhan Older: Oh, sure. They're asking for three to five years.

Sema: (To Murat) It's nothing.

Kathy Older: Nonsense, nonsense. You're going to worry everyone.

Sema: No biggie. We'll take care of it. All I have to do is make a few phone calls. Take someone out to lunch at the most. They're all a bunch of asses.

Orhan Older: (To Brian) Sema has connections, you know. She's a brilliant lawyer.

Brian: Wonderful.

Kathy Older: Isn't that wonderful?

Murat: Why won't you tell me? What's going on?

Orhan Older: It's nothing. Not even worth mentioning.

---

[46] Welcome my beauty. Every time you come you're even more beautiful. What did you bring? Good for you. She's always brings something. She never forgets.

Kathy Older: They're all stupid. The bastards. Sema, have an hors-d'oeuvre, please. Please!

Murat: Why? Why don't you tell me? Why do you treat me like...

Sema: Let it go, let it go.

Orhan Older: Because you just got here and there are more important things and more interesting things to talk about.

Murat: Isn't going to jail important?

Orhan Older: Why should it be? I'll be put away and the rest of you will forget all about me and be happy.

Kathy Older: Oh, no, Orhan, please don't say things like that.

Murat: What? Come on.

Sema: Let it go, Murat.

Orhan Older: Yes, let it go! You're a good daughter, Sema. You understand me completely. (To Brian. Abruptly) Now tell me, Brian. What is this about staying at a hotel?

Brian: Uhm.. We thought it would be a "better" idea.

Orhan Older: Nonsense! Why? It's a ridiculous idea.

Brian: (Looking at Murat) I don't know. We thought that perhaps...

Orhan Older: Nonsense, nonsense. It's stupid. I won't hear of it...

Kathy Older: Let the boy talk, Orhan.

Orhan Older: Why? He has nothing to say.

Kathy Older: Maybe they have a good reason.

Orhan Older: (to Brian) Your mother thinks you have a good reason. What is it?

Murat: We don't want to cause any trouble.

Orhan Older: Trouble? (To Brian) What is he talking about? Does anyone know what he's talking about? Young man, you tell me.

Brian: I think what he's trying to say is...

Orhan Older: Nonsense! I won't accept it!

Sema: You know what he's talking about, for heaven's sake.

Orhan Older: Everyone knows everything except me!

Murat: We didn't want to cause you any discomfort.

Orhan Older: Nonsense!

Kathy Older: What do you mean, dear?

Sema: I don't believe this. Are you actually going to make him say it?

Murat: I thought you might not want people to know that we're here.

Orhan Older: What people, for God's sake? Who are these people?

Sema: Your neighbors, your friends...

Kathy Older: Will you let him talk, both of you...

Orhan Older: Then talk!

Sema: God, I wish I were anywhere but here.

Orhan Older: Be quiet, young lady. Your brother has

something to say.

Brian: Excuse me, can someone tell me where the bathroom...

Orhan Older: Quiet!

Murat: Never mind. It's not important.

Orhan Older: Good. You'll stay here then. You'll bring your bags.

Murat: No! Why are you pushing me? You know very well why. I'm a gay man and I'm here with my lover.

Sema: There, he said it. Are you happy now?

Orhan Older: There's nothing wrong with saying that.

Murat: This is not something you want people to talk about.

Orhan Older: (To Brian) This is very considerate of him, Brian. I'm deeply touched. Murat is a good person. Very sensitive. But we don't care about such people. Let them mind their own business. Tell him Kathy.

Kathy Older: Yes, we don't care! Let them mind their own business.

Orhan Older: In our eyes they do not exist. Because he's our son...

Kathy Older: And we love you.

Orhan Older: ...and he's welcome here. We love him and we're proud of him.

Kathy Older: Yes, we are. (To Brian) We really are.

Murat: Why don't you tell me? Why don't you tell it to my face?

Orhan Older: Because you have hurt our feelings!

Sema: God forbid we should have an evening like a normal family. I'm going to help Kiraz hanım.

Sema exits

Orhan Older: (Cheerfully) Now everyone will relax and I'll fix these young men drinks! We're very happy to be together as a family. Brian, how about a nice glass of rakı?

Brian: No, thanks. If you have some juice or soda...

Orhan Older: Nonsense! Have a real drink.

Murat: Brian doesn't drink, Dad.

Orhan Older: It's our national beverage. Very light, Brian, I promise you.

Murat: He doesn't drink, Dad. I mean how many times do I have to...

Orhan Older: (Hands Brian glass) Here. You can't even taste it.

Brian takes the glass, reluctantly.

Murat: Put that down.

Brian: Murat, it's okay...

Murat: I SAID PUT IT DOWN!

Kathy Older: Oh.

Brian: Take it easy, will you?

Orhan Older: What's the matter? What have I...

Murat: He's an alcoholic, okay? He can't hold a drink.

Kathy Older: I'm so sorry, Brian.

Brian: It's okay. He says that everywhere we go.

Murat: You just don't listen, Dad. Why don't you listen?

Kiraz: (off stage)Yemek hazır, hanımefendi.[47]

Kathy Older: Wonderful! Dinner's ready, everyone. Murat's favorite! Brian, have you tried ram's eggs?

Brian: Someone must tell me where the bathroom is this instant.

Murat: It's down the hall.

Kathy Older: Oh, Turkish tummy. You poor thing.

Orhan Older: (Calling after him) Don't worry about it, Brian. It's psychosomatic!

As they exit, we see Melek at her husband's harem. Evelyn enters.

Evelyn: Melek.

Melek: Evelyn! What are you doing here? How did you...

Evelyn: Shhh. One of the servants let me in.

Melek: (Embracing her) I'm so glad to see you!

Evelyn: How are you Melek?

Melek: Oh, I'm fine, thank you.

Evelyn: We heard you were not well.

Melek: Not well? No, I'm fine.

Evelyn: How are you treated here? How does your husband treat you?

Melek: Very well, thank you.

---

[47] Dinner's ready, my lady.

Evelyn: And your mother-in-law?

Pause. Melek looks down.

Evelyn: (cont'd) Melek?... Please tell me. I've come to help you.

Melek: (cries quietly) She hates me Evelyn. She's always angry at me and she treats me like dirt. And he does too. They've cast me aside like a dirty rag and they don't want to see me or talk to me or have me around. I can't tell you how terrible it's been.

Evelyn: But why? Why are they treating you this way?

Melek: (Crying harder) Because they say that I am barren! That I'm not able to give birth to a son for him. If I can't give birth I'm only a burden on them. Allah has cast me aside and forgotten me.

Evelyn: That's not true, Melek.

Melek: And now my husband has decided to take in another wife! I should have listened to you.

Evelyn: We will get you out of here.

Melek: But how? This is my kismet. I have to endure it.

Evelyn: We'll go to your father.

Melek: He can do nothing for me.

Evelyn: Your father will listen to us, Melek. You will go with me.

Melek sobs. Bedia Older and Osman's house. Kathy greets Anne and Joe at the door. Anne and Joe haven't seen each other in a while and they're all over each other.

Kathy: Hi! Come on in. Nice to see you, Joe.

Joe: (Checking it out) So... This is where you live.

Anne: Yeah. Isn't it nice?

Joe: I don't know. Do *you* think it's nice?

Anne: Of course it's nice. Tell Kathy it's nice.

Joe: (Sarcastically) It's nice.

Kathy: We're going to get our own place soon but for the time being, I don't mind living with my in-laws.

Joe: Yeah. It's very nice.

Kathy: How was your trip?

Joe: It was very nice.

Anne: (Giggling, hanging on to his arm) No, it wasn't. He was late, of course. He hated it.

Kathy: I bet you're glad to see Anne again.

Joe: (Fondling her) Yeah, she's pretty darn nice.

Anne: (Hits him playfully) What's the matter with you, you moron? You think you're so funny.

Joe: (Fondling her as she giggles and squeeks) And Istanbul is nice and this country is great and the people are really really nice and I'm real glad I'm gettin' the hell outta this stinkin' hell!

Kathy: You don't mean that, Joe.

Anne: Sure he does. Hasn't mentioned anything else since he got off the train.

Joe: Yeah. Can't wait to get my hands on a big juicy hamburger and turn on the game and go out with the guys to a real bar. Like I entered a tunnel and all I see is the light at the end: America, here I come. Land of the free, home of the brave...

Anne: (Joe pulls her on his lap) Hill of the numskulls.

Joe: I'm giddy with delight.

Anne: Better be careful what you say in front of Kathy, now, she might clobber you.

Joe: No, she won't. She's an all American girl, the real thing. Aren't you Kathy? You don't become Turkish just because you married a Turkish guy, you know.

Kathy: Do you want a drink, Joe?

Joe: Can you get a real American beer, sweetheart? One sip of that Turkish stuff and I puke.

Anne: You think it's going to get any better if he gets drunk? Where's Orhan anyway?

Kathy: I don't know. He should've been here by now. Do you want a drink, Joe?

Bedia Older: (Sticking in her head) Kathy?

Anne quickly gets off Joe's lap but Bedia Older has already seen her.

Joe: Hey, where're you goin'?

Kathy: Evet Anne?[48]

Bedia Older: Orhan geç kaldı.[49]

Anne: (Goes to Bedia Older) Merhaba Bedia hanım. Nasılsınız?

Bedia Older: Veri gud, veri gud, kızım, hoş geldiniz.

---

[48] Yes mother?
[49] Orhan is late

Kisses her on both cheeks. Goes to Joe. Kisses him as well

Bedia Older: Hoş geldiniz, evladım. Veri gud.

Joe: (Pleasantly) Merhaba, you hideous crone. God, I'm glad I'll never see your ugly Turkish face again.

Anne snorts, trying to keep from laughing.

Bedia Older: (Pleasantly) Veri gud, veri gud. (To Kathy) Kızım siz yemeğe başlayın bari. [50]

Kathy glares at Anne who can barely contain herself

Kathy: Peki, Anne'cigim.[51]

Bedia Older exits

Anne: (Hits Joe, laughing) What's the matter with you? You're such an oaf! That wasn't funny, Joe.

Joe: Oh, lay off. Kathy doesn't mind.

Kathy: You're just a rude, ill bred hick, Joe. That's all.

Joe: Hey, I said, I'm giddy.

Anne: You apologize to Kathy, right now.

Joe: Yeah, I'm sorry.

Kathy: (To Anne) And I don't like her seeing you sitting on his lap either.

Anne: Why not? He's my husband.

Kathy: It's not done, Anne.

Anne: Come on. Are they going to put is in bags and drown us in the Bosphorus or something?

---

[50] My girl, you should start dinner.
[51] Yes, mother.

Kathy: I don't know what happens to you when you get together with him.

Anne: Okay, okay.

Kathy: Orhan's very late. We'd better eat.

Joe: Veri gud, veri gud.

Kathy, Joe and Anne exit. Kathy Older and Murat walk out to the balcony.

Kathy Older: Your father hasn't changed. Still talks and talks. Politics, philosophy, history. As long as someone's listening.

Murat: Or not listening.

Kathy Older: That poor boy! He's sorry he ever left the can.

Murat: He's alright.

Kathy Older: You look good, Murat.

Murat: Thanks, Mom. How are you doing?

Kathy Older: As well as can be expected, I suppose.

Murat: You're finessing me, as usual.

Kathy Older: (Laughs) Not at all. You're terrible.

Murat: Are you happy?

Kathy Older: What? (Chuckles) My. I hadn't thought about that word in years. I don't ask such questions, Murat. I make the best of what I've got. You may or may not appove of that, I don't know. But I'm sure there are others like me in the world who don't allow the same, vast privileges you allow yourself.

Murat: Is that how you feel about me these days?

Kathy Older: It doesn't matter. Your father struggles and I struggle with him. I don't think about whether I'm happy or not.

Murat: Don't you want to go back to the states again, at least for a while?

Kathy Older: Good Lord, no. It costs an arm and a leg.

Murat: Aunt Anne would love to see you.

Kathy Older: Anne? You're joking. She just entered her fifth marriage. She's too busy arranging wedding pictures, she doesn't even remember me.

Murat: You have to go once in a while, Mom. It's your home.

Kathy Older: This is my home, Murat. I can't leave your father alone.

Evelyn and Melek enter the harem. Neyime is there.

Neyime: Melek? My girl, what are you doing here?

Melek: I ran away, Neyime. Evelyn helped me.

Neyime: But this is foolish, my child. They'll come to take you back.

Melek: I want to talk to Papa. Please go get him for me.

Neyime: But what can he do, child?

Evelyn: She can't go back. I won't let you send her back.

Neyime: Alright. I'll go tell him.

Orhan Older and Brian enter living room.

Orhan Older: What do you think, Brian? Is it possible to make a complete break with the past?

Brian: Good question. You mean while "sober?"

Orhan Older: Life's been difficult in our country, Brian. We float through time like a ship with no rudder. Dragged along by whimsical circumstances. It's very frightening. Unfortunately Murat doesn't understand that.

Murat: How much longer can you do this?

Kathy Older: I don't know what you're talking about.

Orhan Older: He doesn't understand the source of my pain, my disillusionment.

Murat: It's as though you don't exist apart from him. He drinks just as much as he always did. He cares little about anyone but himself.

Kathy Older: Now stop that.

Orhan Older: All around the rich are richer and the poor are poorer. We're in an insurmountable debt. And worst of all, we're plagued by the appearance of an islamic elite. The fundamentalists.

Murat: And it's gotten worse. He's in a roomful of people and the only voice he hears is his own.

Kathy Older: Is this why you came, Murat? Just to tell me this? Or do you have something more sinister in mind?

Orhan Older: For the first time since democracy, we see women in veils walk the streets. And why not? Who other than God can help them? I'll tell you who: The Arabs with their "islam" and their "oil money."

Murat: I don't know what I'm saying.

Orhan Older: Like ghosts risen from their graves. They want to put religion back into the schools. they want to close theatres and take down the portraits of Atatürk. We used to worry about the communists and now we have the fundamentalists. Cheers! It's a happy, happy world!

Murat: Once again it's like I'm in a room where the walls move, switch, collapse. Nothing seems right, nothing seems real.

Orhan Older: We have lost hope.

Kathy Older: You can't worry about me, Murat.

Orhan Older: And that's a sad and dangerous thing.

Kathy Older: I never wanted you to.

Murat: Didn't you?

Brian: He wants to make his peace with you, you know. That's why he came.

Orhan Older: I understand that Brian. I understand it perfectly. But the question is: do people change?

Ali Riza Efendi enters the harem.

Ali Riza Efendi: Ah. Mademoiselle Crawley. I should have known. You have put my daughter up to this.

Melek: (Going to him desperately) Papa!

Ali Riza Efendi: (Pushes her away) I thought I had made it clear that you're no longer a welcome guest in my house.

Melek: It isn't Evelyn, Papa. I wanted to escape.

Evelyn: I hope you will listen to your daugher, Ali Rıza Efendi. As you can see, she's quite desperate.

Ali Riza Efendi: I am convinced that if left free of your influence, my daughter will make the right decisions.

Melek: Papa, regardez moi! He hates me, Papa. He's taken another wife! Please don't make me go back!

Ali Riza Efendi does not look at her.

Evelyn: What's the matter, Sir. Are you afraid of looking at your own daughter? Perhaps you are ashamed of the predicament you have assigned her.

Ali Riza Efendi: I am not ashamed of anything. I have always done what is right.

Melek: Écoutez moi, Papa!

Neyime enters.

Neyime: Speak to your daughter, Ali Rıza.

Ali Riza Efendi: (Almost in tears) I can't.

Melek: I know you love me, Papa. I know you don't want me to suffer.

Ali Riza Efendi: (Gently) You are a married woman now, Melek. You have obligations, duties.

Evelyn: Her only obligation is to herself, Monsieur.

Ali Riza Efendi: (Desperately) But I cannot do this. I represent my country. I will lose all credibility. The Sultan will banish me. You must go back, Melek.

Neyime: The world is changing, Ali Rıza.

Ali Riza Efendi: Banished, I tell you! I will be banished!

Melek cries and throws her arms around his neck. Ali Rıza cries with her.

Neyime: Ali Rıza.(Pause) I've never asked you for anything.

You've always given me what was needed and you've always respected me. You're a good man. But every man is not like that. The world is changing. Soon the Sultan might abdicate...

Ali Riza Efendi: No such thing will happen!

Neyime: You know it might happen, Ali Rıza. It is what everyone fears. This country as we have known it for centuries might disappear off the face of the earth.

Ali Riza Efendi: Where do you hear this nonsense? You are only a woman. You don't understand politics.

Neyime: It's almost over for us, my husband. Trust Melek enough to give her the freedom she deserves. Don't send her back, Ali Rıza. I ask you with all my heart.

Ali Riza Efendi turns and leaves.

Melek: Je vous en prie, Papa!

Neyime: Rest easy, my girl. Silence means yes. He cannot say it but he will do it.

Melek: (Hugs her) Thank you, Neyime. Thank you.

Murat and Kathy Older enter the living room.

Orhan Older: Kathy, did you hear that? Brian says he's a tile maker. Works for someone called Yuppie.

Kathy Older: That's nice.

Orhan Older: Good for you, Brian. People should do what they want. When Murat announced he was going to be photographer, we were appalled. "Photography?" we said. It's a hobby not a profession. How can you make a living doing something like that? Didn't we Murat?

Murat: Something like that.

Orhan Older: And when he said he was an "artist" I went into cardiac arrest! But he was smart. He went the way he wanted to go. He's not like the rest of us who are intimidated by other peoples' expectations of us, of what's been drummed into our heads, blah, blah, blah, cowardly stuff.

Sema: (Enters)I sent Kiraz hanım to bed. Anyone ready for coffee?

Orhan Older: Look at me, for example. I became an engineer because my father told me to and I've been miserable all my life! But Murat, he did whatever he wanted to do. He doesn't owe anyone anything. He's free! He's an artist!

Sema: That's right. And it's getting late. Murat do you want to go back to the hotel?

Orhan Older: Bravo, Murat. I'll always respect you for that.

Murat: That's not true.

Orhan Older: (Turns to him) What? What did you say?

Murat: I said, that's not true.

Orhan Older: What? What's not true?

Murat: That you respect me. You've never respected me.

Orhan Older: (Laughs bitterly) Are you calling me a liar, my son? See that Brian? He's calling his father a liar.

Kathy Older: He didn't say that. You misunderstood.

Murat: (Calmly) You're not a liar, Dad. A liar knows he's bending the truth. You're more twisted than that. You actually believe what you say.

Sema: Hey...

Orhan Older: Once again you're talking in riddles. Watch out everyone. The artist has risen!

Murat: It's ridiculous, Dad. We're all pretending everything's fine. That I'm welcome here, that Brian's welcome here.

Orhan Older: You are! Of course you are.

Murat: It's embarrassing, it's a charade!

Orhan Older: Didn't I open the door for you? Didn't I kiss your friend on both cheeks? What more do you want from me? We welcomed you. We embraced you.

Sema: I told you not to come. I told him yesterday.

Murat: You won't even look at my face!

Kathy Older: Oh, stop. We were having such a pleasant evening.

Murat: God. Your daughter has lived with a man you've never met for ten years.

Sema: Oh, my God.

Murat: Do you know it or don't you?

Sema: You're shameless, you know that?

Murat: We're all confused. He must know, we whisper at each other.

Sema: He knows. Of course he knows, you little prick!

Murat: But he won't acknowledge it.

Orhan Older: I don't want to acknowledge it!

Murat: Look at me, Dad.

Orhan Older: I'm looking. What do you want?

Murat: Do you remember what I looked like nine years ago? Did you really look at me then? Did you hear my voice? When you walked up those stairs, your eyes popping out of their sockets, stinking stale of alcohol. Came to find me here, your nostrils flaring, your fists, your knuckles, the way you grabbed me, spat at me, *spat at me!*

Orhan Older: I lost control.

Murat: Lost control? You nearly killed me!

Sema: (To Brian) Why does he deliberately, deliberately go out of his way...

Murat: (About Sema) Hear that voice?

Sema: (To Murat) God, all you do is cause trouble, stir things up like a crazy soup.

Murat: That's your voice. You put it there. Hear the voice coming out of my throat? That's your voice too. When I speak, you hear what you want to hear. When you look at me you see a traitor, someone who's betrayed you. The only things you feel for me are disappointment and anger...

Orhan Older: What is it you want?

Murat: ...and hatred!

Orhan Older: Hatred? How dare you!

Sema: You have to get out of here. (Shoving Murat toward the door) Come on, Murat, let's go!

Orhan Older: STOP! ... I want to hear what he has to say.

Sema: They should leave!

Orhan Older: How dare you tell a father he hates his own son.

Murat: God. I'm not even useful to you anymore.

Orhan Older: What does that mean? Useful?

Murat: I was useful to you because I could be blamed for everything. Your unhappiness, your anger, your moods. Aside from that, you would not acknowledge me.

Orhan Older: You ask too much, Murat.

Orhan enters the apartment in 1952. He's drunk, barely able to stand.

Murat: Don't you remember what you told me before you chased me out of this house? You told me I was an embarrassment to you. That you were ashamed to look at the faces of your friends.

Orhan Older: (explodes) Yes, you were! You were an embarrassment. Then, and now and the whole time you were growing up! I wanted to pretend I didn't know you. I wish I wasn't even related to you.

Kathy, Anne and Joe enter.

Kathy: Orhan, did you forget we had guests?

Orhan Older: Is this what you want to hear?

Joe: Hello, Orhan.

Orhan Older: Now I see you for the first time as a man....

Orhan: Parasites!

Kathy: Orhan!

Orhan Older: Not the man I wanted to see. Not the man I

dreamt.

Orhan: You're not welcome here.

Orhan Older: I dreamt would be my son.

Orhan: Get out of my home.

Kathy: Orhan!

Orhan Older: But look at yourself.

Joe: What's going on, Orhan?

Orhan Older: You're just as lost and angry as I was.

Kathy: You're drunk!

Orhan Older: You're meloncholy. Burdened by your own life.

Orhan: They turned me down, those American bastards!

Orhan Older: You accuse me of not looking at you, of not hearing your voice.

Orhan: And he's the one who told them not to hire me!

Joe: There was a good reason for that.

Orhan Older: How can I hear it, Murat?

Orhan: Tell him to get out of my house.

Orhan Older: All it tells me is what went wrong with my own life.

Kathy: I'll tell him no such thing.

Orhan Older: I was a young man full of optimism and promise...

Kathy: You'll apologize!

Orhan Older: ... and today I'm a failure. A failure!

Joe: You have no experience, Orhan.

Orhan Older: And you. You're where I failed the most.

Orhan: He didn't want a Turkish man working in his firm.

Joe: That's not true...

Orhan: We let them build their refinery.

Orhan Older: I can't look at you without wincing.

Orhan: They've breathed our air, eaten our bread...

Orhan Older: Your voice makes me shudder.

Orhan: And you act like you've done us a favor!

Orhan Older: But how can I escape you? My own son!

Orhan: (Advancing toward Joe) We don't need your charity.

Joe: Hey!

Orhan: (Lunging toward him) So get out. Get out!

Kathy gets in between.

Kathy: Stop that!

Orhan Older: You think you're so superior, Murat.

Joe: Let's get out of here.

Joe and Anne exit

Orhan Older: What makes you think you're so superior?

Kathy: I don't know who you are.

Orhan Older: What have you found in your life that I haven't?

Sinan Ünel

Kathy exits

Murat: I've found Brian. I've found my intuition.

Orhan Older: So have I! Look at her. She's my intuition, she's my soul. She breathes for me, walks for me...

Sema: Mixes your drinks.

Murat: You're just tormented by some ancestral fatalism. You're angry all the time, you hate your work, you can't be proud of anything or anyone...

Orhan Older: What do you want me to do, Murat? Kill myself?

Murat: (Silence. An uncomfortable moment. Then:) Yes. Yes. You always threaten to do it, but you won't just do it, you want to prolong it, make everybody watch.

Kathy Older: Oh, my God.

Murat: Why don't you just do it and save the rest of us this burden, this, this unbearable guilt.

Kathy Older: Murat! How could you?

Murat: Why don't you do it, Dad?

Kathy Older: Shut up! Shut up!

Brian: (Touching him) Murat...

Murat: (Abruptly) Don't touch me! (Brian pulls away. Murat looks at him) Don't touch me. (To Orhan Older) ALL I WANT IS TO FORGIVE YOU. THAT'S ALL I NEED FROM YOU NOW.

Orhan Older: I'm very tired.

Kathy Older: Orhan, please...

Orhan Older: I want to go to bed. Sleep this night away. Good night Brian. Meeting you has been a pleasure.

Brian: Good night.

Orhan Older leaves

Brian: (cont'd) Will I be okay in a cab?

Murat: Brian, I'm sorry.

Brian: It's okay.

Sema: You'll be fine.

Murat: Don't go.

Brian: I'll see you at the hotel, okay?

Brian leaves

Kathy Older: You're just destructive, Murat. Are you proud that once again you've toppled a house of cards?

Murat: Year after year I watched you as you became more resigned, as though your bones shrank, as you became smaller and bitter. Don't you see what's happened to you?

Kathy Older: Stop. You and I both had in our lives that moment, that all important decision that would change everything irreversibly. We're lucky about that. We are. Did you know how it would turn out? I didn't.

A servamt enters, running.

Servant: Melek Sultan, Melek Sultan!

Kathy Older: But we both took the plunge, didn't we?

Melek: What is it, boy?

Servant: Refik Aga told us. The Sultan has abdicated! He's left the country on a British ship!

Melek: My God. Where's Papa?

Melek runs off.

Kathy Older: You left this country to build yourself a life we couldn't understand or accept. That was courageous, perhaps. But now you don't want to take the responsibility.

Kathy enters.

Kathy: How could you do that? Are you a lunatic?

Kathy Older: My time came forty years ago.

Orhan: Have you seen the paper today, my beautiful American wife?

Melek: (Running) Papa!

Kathy Older: Forty years.

Kathy: I hate it when you're like this.

Orhan: Of course not. My poor wife does not read Turkish.

Melek: Papa!

Kathy: I won't let you do this anymore.

Kathy Older: Perhaps marrying your father was the best thing I ever did.

Orhan: Look at the headline.

Melek finds Javid.

Melek: Javid, where's Papa?

Kathy Older: Or perhaps it was my biggest mistake.

Melek: (Shaking him) Tell me Javid!

Javid nods in a direction. Melek runs.

Orhan: The president of Turkey is in the US just now. As a welcome guest of who else? President Eisenhower.

Kathy Older: But how many women my age can say differently?

Kathy: I won't put up with it. You won't come home drunk like this again.

Kathy Older: There are no right decisions, Murat.

Orhan: Look. People are cheering him on the streets of New York. American carpets are laid underneath his feet. And do you know why?

Kathy: I don't care! This is all you babble about when you're drunk!

Orhan: Because we struggle for democracy! We fight for the same principles as America.

Kathy: Who cares? Who gives a damn?

As this is happening, Melek spots Neyime sitting on the floor, crying. Afraid of what she'll find, Melek slowly walks toward her.

Orhan: We're guardians against the evil of communism! Do you know what that means?

Kathy: Who cares what America thinks about Turkey? Who the hell cares?

Orhan: Do you know what that means?

Kathy Older: Any marriage is a mistake on some level. How could I have known that your father would SPROUT into such a masterpiece? That MY SON WOULD BECOME SUCH AN ARROGANT, UNFORGIVING SHIT! THAT I WOULD BE TRAPPED, TRAPPED...

Kathy: Shut up! Shut up! I don't care what it means!

Orhan slaps Kathy, hard. She falls. Kathy Older gasps.

Murat: Mom, are you alright?

Sema: Mother!

Melek: Neyime?

Orhan goes after Kathy. Lifts her up and hits her again. She screams and flies across the room. Kathy Older gasps again, trying to breathe.

Sema: God! Get her some water, quick!

Orhan goes after Kathy. Hits her again. Melek looks up to see her father's body hanging from a rope. She screams. Out of breath, Orhan stops. Kathy's crouched against the wall, covering herself. Murat rushes to Kathy Older with water. She drinks.

Murat: What happened? Are you okay?

Kathy Older: I'm fine. Don't worry about me. I'm fine.

Sema: God. I'm calling the doctor.

Kathy Older: No. I'm fine. Find your father for me.

Javid appears behind Melek and Neyime.

Murat: Call the doctor. Go on. Call the doctor.

Kathy Older: No! Find your father.

Orhan: It means that we are equals. And that we are to be treated as equals.

Javid holds Melek. Bedia Older enters, sees Kathy crouched on the floor. She goes to her and leans next to her, trying to console her.

Bedia Older: Ah, ağlama güzelim. Erkek milleti böyledir, zalimdirler evlâdım. Kalk, kalk, hadi. Üzme kendini yavrum. Bak bana bakayım. Vay eşşek, nasılda vurmus yüzüne. Yazık sana evladım. [52]

Melek and Kathy continue to cry during the following. Bedia Older wipes Kathy's face and continues to speak to her in Turkish.

Kathy Older: I have not become the person I thought I would become. Have you heard anything more senseless than that?

Murat: Does he still hit you?

Kathy Older: No. We've moved way beyond that. We have texture now. We've evolved into a stranger organism. We've devised peculiar methods to survive together, my dear husband and I. And we're happy about that. Is that okay with you?

Sema re-enters.

Sema: He's gone.

Murat: What do you mean? Where?

Sema: Through the back door. Who knows?

Kathy Older: I do. That eternal ferry again. He's been doing that lately.

Murat: I'll go find him.

Murat exits.

Sema: (To Kathy Older) I don't like that thing that just happened. That chest thing or whatever it was.

Kathy Older: I'm fine. It was nothing.

Sema: You almost couldn't breathe. That wasn't nothing. It

---

[52] Don't cry, my darling. Men are like that, they're cruel, my child. Get up, get up, come. Don't be so sad. Look at me. That ass, how he hit your face. I pity you my child.

frightened the hell out of me. When were you at the doctor last?

Kathy Older: Last week.

Sema: God, you're lying.

Kathy Older: I'll make an appointment tomorrow.

Sema: You and him both and your health. It's my biggest fear. I'm going to walk in one day and find two stubborn corpses.

Kathy Older: Perhaps we should meet your friend soon.

Sema: My friend.

Kathy Older: You know. The one you never told us about and we never knew about except we did.

Sema: Sorry. He wouldn't do very well in this milieu. Being not particularly social in disposition.

Kathy Older: Maybe dinner at the club some night.

Sema: He's married, okay? We'll talk about it some other time.

Kathy Older: Okay. We'll look forward to that.

Lights dim low. The Bosphorus Ferry. Orhan Older looks out to the shore. Murat is behind him.

Murat: Dad.

Orhan Older: I'm trying to find something I've lost, Murat. Is it a scent? A sound? Something I once touched? You and I are alike that way, searching for the same thing. Do you think you'll find it?

Orhan appears

Murat: I don't know.

Orhan Older: I wish I could help you, Murat. But once you assimilate the ideas of another country, once you understand the essence, you have no alternative but to be alienated from your own. I stepped through that threshold when I was young and I've never found my way back.

Orhan: God. What have I done?

Orhan Older: You'll never forgive me, Murat. You know that don't you?

Orhan: What have I done?

Murat: Yes, I will.

Orhan Older: Look. The seagulls are flying low. There's going to be a storm.

Orhan sobs. Hotel room. Morning. Kathy, Anne and Joe.

Joe: It's impossible! We can't leave her here with a man who beats her.

Anne: Kathy?

Kathy: Don't come near me. I don't want anyone touching me.

Joe: You're not staying, Kathy. You're going home with us.

Anne: You don't understand, Joe.

Joe: What? What's there to understand?

Anne: She's pregnant.

Joe: (to Kathy)Does he know?

Kathy shakes her head no.

Joe: (cont'd) Look. We won't even tell him. He's been sitting out in the hall since last night. All we'll tell him is that you're going home with us.

Anne: Leave us alone, Joe.

Joe: Don't do this to her!

Anne motions him away. He leaves.

Anne: I'm not going to tell you what to do. My heart is breaking. I'll help you raise the child if you come with us. But I won't let you go live with Mom and be a burden on her.

Kathy: I know.

Anne: Do you want to see him?

Kathy: In a little while.

Kathy goes to the bathroom. At the harem, Melek and Javid.

Javid: You must talk to Maman, Melek. We can't leave Bedia here.

Melek: There's nothing I can do, Javid.

Javid: Yes there is! Maman will listen to you.

Evelyn enters.

Melek: Evelyn? What are you doing here?

Evelyn: I came as soon as I heard, Melek.

Javid: What business do you have in our house? No one wants to talk to you.

Melek: Javid, go to your room. You've been nothing but an annoyance today.

Javid leaves, angrily.

Evelyn: I promise you, I didn't know it would come to this.

Melek: You shouldn't have come, Evelyn.

Evelyn: I'm so sorry, Melek. What will you do?

Melek: We think we'll go to Nice. Several of our cousins are going there. Neyime says we can give french lessons. Although I don't know why the french would pay to learn their own language. The only other thing I know how to do is embroidery. Do you think the french women would be interested in that?

Evelyn: Please allow me to help you.

Neyime enters, followed by Javid.

Javid: Maman, I beg you to reconsider. Bedia is my only friend!

Neyime: Impossible, my son. Don't insist anymore.

Javid: She knows no other family. She's heartbroken.

Neyime: Good afternoon, Mademoiselle Crawley.

Evelyn: Good afternoon.

Bedia runs in, throws herself at Neyime's feet.

Bedia: Ne olur, hanım Sultan, benide götürün! [53]

Neyime: Stand up, Bedia. Don't make a scene.

Javid: She's been faithful to you all her life, Maman!

Neyime: We can't afford her, don't you understand? We can't pay for her food, her clothing. You have your freedom, my girl. We've selected a good husband for you.

Bedia: (Sobbing) I won't be a burden, I promise. I'll eat out of trash cans. I'll beg in the streets.

---

[53] Please my lady, take me with you.

Evelyn: (Trying to lift her) Bedia, get up, Bedia, please...

Bedia spits at Evelyn.

Bedia: Don't touch me, you evil woman!

Melek: Bedia! How dare you?

Bedia: I'm a free woman now! I can spit on anyone I like!

She runs off.

Neyime: I'm sorry about that, Mademoiselle Crawley.

Javid: I'm not! It's the least she deserves!

Melek: Javid!

Javid: How can you still stand here, have you no shame? Your evil government is calling us traitors. We're sent to exile as though we're an embarrassment, as though six hundred years of rule never happened!

Evelyn: I'm sorry, Javid, I did not know.

Javid: Liar! Liar! How could you have not known? Are you proud of what you've done?

Evelyn: Yes, I am. I'm very proud.

Javid: Look down Süleyman the Magnificent and Noble Yavuz! Look what's happened to your supreme empire! I don't want to go to Europe! Papa did the right thing! I want to kill myself like Papa!

He runs off. Javid Older is there.

Javid Older: Look down Süleyman the Magnificent and Noble Yavuz.

Melek: Good bye, Evelyn. Perhaps I'll see you again one day.

Evelyn: No, Melek, no. I'm not proud. I'm lost. I didn't know what was at stake.

Javid Older: Look what's happened to your supreme empire.

Melek: I was naive, Evelyn, you were right about that. It was naive of me to think we could be friends.

Evelyn: Melek...

Melek leaves. Evelyn is alone. Javid Older speaks to the audience. Kathy reenters the hotel room.

Javid Older: Your grandchildren are chased off without packing their underwear. This was the saddest day of our lives. To leave our beautiful Istanbul, the magnificent tulips, the sad melodies, our sunsets over the Bosphorus. All in one day gone. It was more than any of us could bear.

Murat enters the hotel room.

Murat: Brian?

Javid Older: We were lost in France, like orphans without food or shelter. After one year in Nice, my beautiful sister Melek shut her eyes to life. After her death I had no reason to live. But I went on. My mother married a wealthy French diplomat and nearly twenty years after our departure, I was permitted to return to my beloved city again.

Brian comes out of the bathroom.

Brian: A miracle has happened. I haven't shat in one full hour.

Javid Older: But I was old now. I was poor, homeless...

Brian: Are you okay?

Javid Older: I found my childhood friend, my kind Bedia...

Murat: I'm ashamed.

Javid Older: And she took me in. Without her kindness I would not be alive today.

Brian: You came and you faced your predicament Murat. Nobody does this without guilt.

Murat: He doesn't scare me anymore. Is that a loss? Is every goddamn thing a loss?

Brian: Let's go to bed. You'll feel better in the morning.

Orhan enters the hotel room. Kathy is there.

Orhan: Words cannot convey the way I feel, Kathy. I'm afraid. Joe says you'll return to the States. Tell me it's not true.

Kathy: My mother lived her whole life angry at one man. I won't let that happen to me.

Orhan: That man wasn't me. I don't know where he came from. I'm not like that, Kathy. You know that.

Brian exits to the bathroom.

Kathy: What are you like? What if I never learn who you are?

Orhan Older appears.

Orhan Older: I was drunk.

Kathy: That's not an excuse.

Orhan: I'm sorry.

Murat: (Sitting up in bed) Brian?

Kathy: I left my country for you.

Orhan Older: I know.

Murat: Brian, where are you?

Kathy: I changed my life. I gave up everything.

Orhan Older: I know.

Orhan: I know.

Murat: (At bathroom door) Are you in there, Brian? Are you sick again?

Javid Older: The night before our departure...

Orhan Older: We did not become the people we thought we would become.

Orhan: Did we, Kathy?

Javid Older: That night I had a dream.

Murat: I'm scared.

Brian: (Unseen) Don't be scared.

Murat: Where are you? I can't see you.

Orhan: Forgive me.

Kathy: No.

Murat: Brian?

Javid Older: A very strange dream.

Javid: (Appears) I'm here.

Kathy: I'll never forgive you for the way you made me feel.

Murat: You're not Brian. Who are you?

Kathy: Rotten, putrid inside...

Javid: I'm your loss, I'm your sadness.

Kathy: All of these years, I've never forgiven you for that.

Orhan: Oh, God.

Orhan Older: I know.

Murat: But why? Why are you sad?

Javid: I'll never be whole again.

Murat: Don't say that. You don't know what the future holds.

Kathy: And I can't forgive myself. For not leaving you. Now.

Murat: Your sadness is a gift. Soon you'll be free. You'll overcome destiny. You'll make your own future.

Kathy: Why won't I leave you? Now?

Javid: But who will I be? Will I ever know again who I am?

Orhan Older: If you met me today, Kathy, would you still marry me?

Murat: Yes, you will.

Kathy: Yes.

Murat: Have courage, Javid. You belong everywhere.

Murat kisses Javid.

Orhan: I'm your destiny.

Kathy: Oh, yes.

Orhan Older: You are everything to me.

Murat: I release you now. So go. Now. Go.

Javid leaves

Javid Older: The next morning I woke with an unfamiliar feeling. I couldn't remember the dream. But I had hope. What was the dream I'd had. What was setting me free?

Behind him, Melek and Neyime appear. Melek hums to the music. A servant helps them dress in western clothes.

Melek: Listen. He plays so beautifully that Javid.

Neyime: Yes.

Melek: Are you afraid?

Neyime: No.

Melek: Look I've bought us hats.

Neyime: Ah. Yes.

Melek: Aren't they pretty?... Come on. Put it on.

Morning. Murat, half dressed, is taking pictures on the balcony. Brian enters.

Brian: Okay, I paid the bill. That cute guy's coming up to take the bags.

Murat: Just one more minute.

Brian: The whole staff is gathered in the lobby, waiting to see us off. It's so strange, yet so... *thrilling!* (Comes out to the balcony) You're not even dressed yet.

Murat: How long do we have?

Brian: Don't worry, we have time.

Murat: How long?

Brian: All day. I don't know. Or all month.

Melek: You look beautiful, Neyime.

Brian looks inside. The Porter's entered, waiting for instructions. Brian waves him away.

Brian: Bırak Ahmet. Teşekkür ederim.[54]

The Porter smiles, nods and leaves. Murat continues to snap pictures.

Evelyn: Once again, I look out of my room in this European hotel, that I have, somehow, grown to like over the years. My heart is breaking, Melek. But I can't help but think I've done all the right things. Under my feet is the young country that has emerged from the ruins of an old, sinking state. The sick man of Europe has been resurrected as a new nation, looking to the future. It is a true miracle. But how can I be sure? Will this hopeful nation survive as a western country? Will you, my beautiful angel survive as a western woman? Only the future, the frightening, unfamiliar future will show us.

Javid Older continues to play a sad Turkish tune. Melek sings. Murat takes another picture. Blackout.

END OF PLAY

---

54 Leave it, Ahmet. Thank you.

Sinan Ünel's plays have been produced at: The Huntington
Theatre Company, The Long Wharf Theater, The Arcola
Theatre (London), Boston Playwrights' Theatre, The Lark
Theatre Company (New York), The Gate Theatre (London),
Provincetown Theatre Company, Provincetown
Theatreworks, Landes-theater (Germany), Theater Kosmos
(Austria), Theatre at Boston Court (Pasadena, CA). Sinan has
been awarded The John Gassner Memorial Award, The Daryl
Roth Creative Spirit Award, and a Calderwood Fellowship
from the Huntington Theatre Company. His script Race
Point is the winner of the 2001 New Century Writer Award
for best screenplay.. Sinan divides his time between New
York and Cape Cod, and teaches at Lesley University.

www.sinanunel.com

Other plays by Sinan Ünel

Chatal
New Life
Pathétique
Single Lives
A Mad Person's Chronicle of a Miserable Marriage
The Lost Gospels of Blankenburg
Thalassa, My Heart
Portals
The Three of Cups

47463275R00082

Made in the USA
Middletown, DE
25 August 2017